"You are very deeply loved,"
says the Lord."
Malachi 1:2

Enjoy Fernandina Beach

Loraine Pakkala

2017

Also by Lorraine Pakkala:

Random Harvest: Weekly columns from 1980 – 1983

PTL Devotionals for 1984 – 1986

Yea God!

Uplift, Collaboration with Barbara Delinsky
and Breast Cancer Survivors

# Land of Forgetfulness

## Adapting Through a Journey of Alzheimer's

### Lorraine Pakkala

WestBow Press
A DIVISION OF THOMAS NELSON
& ZONDERVAN

Copyright © 2017 Lorraine Pakkala.

All rights reserved. No part of this book may be used or reproduced by any means, graphic, electronic, or mechanical, including photocopying, recording, taping or by any information storage retrieval system without the written permission of the author except in the case of brief quotations embodied in critical articles and reviews.

This book is a work of non-fiction. Unless otherwise noted, the author and the publisher make no explicit guarantees as to the accuracy of the information contained in this book and in some cases, names of people and places have been altered to protect their privacy.

The events in this book are real experiences. Except for family members, the other people mentioned have fictitious names. The exception is my husband 'Andy' where I chose to use a loved nickname.

KJV - Scripture quotes are taken from the King James Version of the Bible.

All Scriptures are from The Living Bible except for King James versions indicated by a *KJ*.

WestBow Press books may be ordered through booksellers or by contacting:

WestBow Press
A Division of Thomas Nelson & Zondervan
1663 Liberty Drive
Bloomington, IN 47403
www.westbowpress.com
1 (866) 928-1240

Because of the dynamic nature of the Internet, any web addresses or links contained in this book may have changed since publication and may no longer be valid. The views expressed in this work are solely those of the author and do not necessarily reflect the views of the publisher, and the publisher hereby disclaims any responsibility for them.

Any people depicted in stock imagery provided by Thinkstock are models, and such images are being used for illustrative purposes only. Certain stock imagery © Thinkstock.

ISBN: 978-1-5127-6618-9 (sc)
ISBN: 978-1-5127-6619-6 (hc)
ISBN: 978-1-5127-6617-2 (e)

Library of Congress Control Number: 2016919686

Print information available on the last page.

WestBow Press rev. date: 03/06/2017

# Dedication

This book was written to be of assistance to those receiving the shattering news of a loved one entering or already in the throes of Alzheimer's. When the sad reality of my husband's diagnosis was confirmed, I searched for a book to help me in the day-to-day routine to just get by. I found books with reams of statistics and warnings of terminal certainty, but nothing helpful for coping on a daily basis. I'm sharing here some of the coping mechanisms that were helpful to me. Most of the input is taken from my journals that I kept to relieve my own fears.

I lived through the changes of having a strong, authoritative husband who became a willful four-year-old, throwing gigantic tantrums and suffering odd obsessions and hallucinations.

I collaborated on *Uplift* – a book designed to help women facing breast cancer. Reading the book is similar to sitting down with a friend for a frank discussion of the trials and pitfalls of breast cancer. My hope is that *Land of Forgetfulness* will be of similar help for wives, husbands, and anyone else coping with the disappearance of a loved one into Alzheimer's.

One of my lifesavers during this difficult time was attending meetings of the local caregivers group. We shared each other's problems and solutions. Sometimes just the knowledge we weren't alone was helpful. Since the death of my husband, the leader of this group, Debra Dombkowski, has urged me to continue to attend meetings. As she puts it, "Your expertise is invaluable in helping those still trying to cope."

Each caregiver will experience obstacles unique to their loved one. Hopefully, some of my techniques will be of help on this sad journey. There are over five million people in the U.S. currently living with Alzheimer's.

That number is expected to more than double by 2050. This is a very scary statistic indeed. There is a small measure of comfort in knowing you are not alone. My hope is this book will give you that measure of comfort. I've been there and lived through it. Let me share your burden.

# Acknowledgments

Many thanks to my beloved daughters, Cheryl and Shelly, who contributed so much to *Land Of Forgetfulness*. Theirs was a team effort of designing the cover, copy editing, and graphic design. They are upbeat, smart, and always willing to be helpful. Not the least of their attributes, they are fun people.

I owe a deep gratitude to Tiffany Wilson, a professional writer and incidentally my granddaughter, for her help in what to include and what to exclude. She also painfully yanked out my excessive use of commas. She kept me focused on the basic purpose of *Land of Forgetfulness*, which is to encourage others walking through the uneven terrain of daily life with Alzheimer's.

I want to extend many thanks to my son, Walter, for the endless hours of nature walks and for just spending time with my husband during the darkest days. Thanks to his wife, Brenda, for the many meals and conversations she so graciously provided. Together they provided an oasis of normalcy that was so lacking in my life at that time.

I extend love and gratitude to the Fernandina Beach caregivers group for their profound influence on the content of this book. They helped me sort out the things that are relevant to on-going caregiving and especially encouraged me to put down on paper what we lived - and are living - in our efforts to honor our loved ones with dignity and love. These loyal friends have freely given their input and contributed greatly to give balance to my perspective. I stand in awe of the selflessness of these people. There is no tribute large enough to portray the bravery, steadfast love, and faithfulness of this unsung army. They have been invaluable to me as I've tried to put down on paper the daily struggles we have each faced.

The events in this book are real experiences. Except for family members, people mentioned have been given fictitious names. For my husband 'Andy' I chose to use a loved nickname.

# Foreword

Dementia *is* "The Land of Forgetfulness."

This book is written by an amazingly brave and courageous woman who learned, lived, and adapted through a long journey of Alzheimer's Dementia with her husband. (Alzheimer's is a type of Dementia).

She writes from her heart, telling us about some of the trials and tribulations she and her husband encountered throughout their journey battling this terminal and devastating disease. Lorraine hopes that by reading this book, you will have a closer insight into the reality of "a day in the life" of Alzheimer's Dementia and find helpful hints in how to deal with your own situation living with this horrific disease.

She shows us what their lives were like and how she adapted minute-by-minute, day-by-day. She worked very hard at making sure that her dear husband's life was lived safely and comfortably, with normalcy, dignity, and respect. She shows us how simple and invaluable techniques can help us deal with this disease.

This is a unique and easy-to-read book for all caregivers that provides support and understanding in caring for your loved one with dementia.

Reading this book reminds us that caregivers and those afflicted with dementia are not alone. Even though we often question what the best treatment or course of action is, the love, care, and effort that we show is invaluable in providing a high quality standard of life for those suffering from Alzheimer's.

Although each person is different, and dementia manifests itself in a multitude of ways, we can help each other by recognizing the similarities between our situations and share the best practices that we have learned and developed.

Dealing with the constantly-evolving challenges of being a caregiver for someone with dementia is a daunting task. Knowing your loved one and dealing with the challenges on a day-to-day and step-by-step basis makes the situation much more manageable. Lorraine's book provides the real-world guidance necessary to help us feel less overwhelmed.

I cried (and thankfully laughed) while reading this book, as it really expresses what life with dementia is like.

I hope that when you read this book you, too, will find comfort, support, humor, and a few good tips in dealing with your everyday situation caring for your loved one with dementia. By learning from and supporting each other, we will not only manage, but defeat this terrible affliction.

Written by:

Debra Dombkowski LPN, CDP
Licensed Practical Nurse & Certified Dementia Practitioner
Nassau County Council on Aging Adult Day HealthCare Manager
Nassau County Council on Aging Caregiver Support Group Facilitator

# Contents

Dedication .......................................................................................... v
Acknowledgments .......................................................................... vii
Foreword .......................................................................................... ix

Chapter 1   Beginning Land of Forgetfulness ................................ 1
Chapter 2   The Watch ...................................................................... 6
Chapter 3   Key West ....................................................................... 14
Chapter 4   Rage ............................................................................... 22
Chapter 5   Wandering .................................................................... 28
Chapter 6   Hurdles ......................................................................... 46
Chapter 7   Caregivers .................................................................... 53
Chapter 8   Sex ................................................................................. 60
Chapter 9   Shopping Trip ............................................................. 66
Chapter 10  Nursing Home ............................................................. 72
Chapter 11  At the Hospital ........................................................... 79

Epilogue    Two Years Later .......................................................... 85
Coping Clues .................................................................................. 87

# Chapter One

## Beginning Land of Forgetfulness

### PSALM 88:12

In our nearly twenty years of marriage, my husband, Andy, and I took several journeys to Australia, England, Scotland, and Canada. But, there was one eight-year-long trip we never intended or anticipated—a trip to the Land of Forgetfulness, known as Alzheimer's.

It had taken a jolt for me to realize that all was not well with Andy. He was a Certified Public Accountant retired from a lifelong career with a major oil company. He was in full charge of our household accounts. The awakening realization came when Andy came to me and asked me to take over the accounts. His arms full of checkbooks, bills, and bank deposit slips, he asked me to hold out my hands and take over. "I don't know what's happening to me, but I just can't make sense of it anymore. Things are just fuzzy." I did a quick calculation: what had formerly been a two-hour reconciliation at the end of each month had become an all-day session ending in this final giving up.

With growing apprehension, I responded to an offer in the local paper for a publication about the early warning signs of the most devastating disorder affecting older people: Alzheimer's disease. I received "The Seven Warning Signs of Alzheimer's Disease." The list included:

1. Asking the same question over and over again.
2. Repeating the same story, word for word, again and again.

3. Forgetting how to cook, or how to make repairs, or how to play cards – activities that were previously done with ease and regularity.
4. Losing one's ability to pay bills or balance a checkbook.
5. Getting lost in familiar surroundings or misplacing household objects.
6. Neglecting to bathe, or wearing the same clothes over and over again, while insisting that they have taken a bath or that their clothes are still clean.
7. Relying on someone else, such as a spouse, to make decisions or answer questions they previously would have handled themselves. *(Source: University of South Florida Suncoast Alzheimer's & Gerontology Center).*

Of the seven warning signs, I had to answer yes to six of them. The only one that didn't apply to Andy was number six, neglecting to bathe and wearing the same clothes day after day. In fact, I had to be vigilant or he'd take several showers a day.

As the reality of "the list" washed over me, so too did a deep despair. These were the first warning signs that my beloved was sinking in quicksand that I couldn't pull him out of. He was still a delightful companion, loving and thoughtful, but there was a subtle daily slippage. Maybe not so subtle, as he asked question after question. "What time is it? What day is it? Where is my wallet?" These constantly asked questions confirmed my worst fears.

I later learned Alzheimer's often afflicts the most brilliant among us. After reading through reams of books on the subject, my own take on Alzheimer's boiled down to this: a plaque forms in the brain similar to tangled yarn. It grows and expands, lessening brain function as it grows. Doctors don't know when or how it starts or how to stop it.

I lived the nitty-gritty, day-to-day of adjusting from having a brilliant, self-sufficient husband to undertaking shepherding, coaxing, cajoling, and sometimes even tricking him into taking his daily pills, getting dressed, and eating meals, all the while answering a million questions a day: *What day is it? What time is it? Where are we?*

Later, we consulted with the local authority on Alzheimer's disease, Dr. P. He conducted his own evaluation, asking Andy: "What year is it?

Who is president? What is your address? What is your phone number?" Andy answered wrong on every question.

Dr. P looked me sternly in the eyes and told me emphatically, "Alzheimer's is a terminal disease; at present, there is no cure. There are a few medications out there, but at best they only delay onset by a few months. Understand, you never win an argument with an Alzheimer's patient; it's best just to agree with them. Sorry to tell you this, but you'll probably have to learn to lie. If he says it's Friday on a Monday, just agree. An Alzheimer's patient is always right. If you understand that, you'll save yourself hours of frustration. I like Alzheimer's patients because they never hold a grudge. With a twenty minute attention-span, you can't hold a grudge."

As the chilling cloak of the certainty that Andy had Alzheimer's settled around me, I felt I was at the top of a deep abyss and could fall down into it any minute. That dismal foundation marked the beginning of our grim journey.

## SEVEN YEARS INTO THE JOURNEY

I sank gratefully into bed. It seemed every bone and fiber of my body was exhausted, stretched thin almost to the breaking point. Especially my brain. If brains can be exhausted, mine surely was.

Not so Andy. As usual when I was ready to clock out, he was just getting revved up. Sitting up yoga-style on his bed he announced, "I have a question."

Trying to ignore him, I burrowed deeper into my soft pillow. All I wanted was the sweet release of sleep. I glanced at my comforting pillow, thinking, *Oh no! Not another question.* Every twenty minutes, all day, every day, question after question. Today had been especially exhausting. "What time is it? What day is it? Where is my sister Lilli? Can't she go with us on our walk? Where's my wallet?" I knew there'd be no rest for me until he'd asked the last question.

Looking truly puzzled, he continued, "I know I was married to Milli and she died. Then, I was married to Lorraine and I don't know what happened to her. My question is, who are you?"

I sat up. "I'm Lorraine, your wife."

He snorted loudly in denial, "Oh no! I know you're not. Lorraine was a cheerful person, lots of fun and always laughing. Not you! You are bossy and grouchy. You never laugh or have any fun with me. Who *are* you?"

Even in my exhaustion, I had to acknowledge I wasn't the same Lorraine he'd married. As drastically as Alzheimer's disease had changed Andy, it had just as drastically changed me. He was right – I wasn't the same person. I'd become a bossy grouch. I realized Alzheimer's was taking a daily toll on *me*. Like water eroding a stone – drip by steady drip, day by day. Nothing noticeable at first, but at the end of seven years I had eroded from a cheerful, fun-loving person to a bossy grouch.

## ALZHEIMER'S IS NOBODY'S FAULT

Early on in Andy's disability, I'd determined to be honest about his affliction. After all, a broken mind is similar to a broken leg – nobody's fault, not even an assessment on intelligence. A broken brain is just that, a brain that no longer functions correctly. I've met families who deny a problem exists and try to answer questions quickly to hide the problem. In short, they treat Alzheimer's as something to be ashamed of. There's much less pressure on the family and the patient to admit there's a problem. I decided with all my resolve to be honest about Andy's disability. I also discovered that, by my being honest about Alzheimer's, others opened up to disclose a family member or close friend who had also experienced the disease. Alzheimer's has universally touched lives, leaving families to grieve over a former brilliant loved one reduced to child-like dependence. Realize early-on there is no stigma attached to Alzheimer's. Like any disease, the experts know very little about why it happens or why some contract it and others don't. Nothing in lifestyle or behavior is a known trigger for the disease.

I remembered my friend who attended lovingly to her Alzheimer's afflicted mother. She often said, "She doesn't know who I am, but I know who she is." Sometimes that's all we can do. Just know who they really are.

Andy often complained that the water heater was broken and he'd had to take a cold shower. One day, it occurred to me he couldn't be right - I'd had a hot shower just a half hour before. I realized he'd forgotten how the single-handled faucet worked. In addition, he no longer knew the day, month, or year and asked hourly about it. I partially solved this by putting the day of the week on a large banner on the refrigerator. He sometimes checked out the newspaper to affirm the day, as he often argued with me about the day posted on the fridge. But most of the time it helped. I realized he was trying to find an anchor to hook onto – time that most of us take for granted in our daily lives.

At this stage he was often enraged, exhibiting signs of extreme agitation. The most extreme unrest usually occurred in the late afternoon. Later I learned the timing of his agitation was common, known as "Sundown Syndrome." Sometimes he couldn't remember names of grandchildren, how to turn on and off the TV, our phone number, or our address.

Reality crashed in! My brilliant Andy was no longer the steady, dependable rock I'd looked to and depended on. I recalled the Lord's promise when I'd gone through breast cancer years earlier. Learning I had breast cancer, I'd totally panicked. I bombarded the Lord with prayer. My very foundation was rocked. Frantically, I begged the Lord for assurance. Opening my Bible, it seemed like these words were almost neon-lit: "Yes, God alone is my Rock, my rescuer, defense and fortress. Why then should I be tense with fear when troubles come?" *(Psalm 62:2)*

Andy, my strong rock, was crumbling. I was losing not only his loving companionship, but ultimately him. Yet again, the Lord had to remind me *He* alone was my Rock.

# Chapter Two

# The Watch

I was twelve years healed from a sad divorce. I was so determined never to marry again, I'd asked my sister Jennie to chain me to the bedpost if I ever even *thought* of marrying again.

Then, enter Andy. His beloved wife Milli had died unexpectedly at the age of only 59. He, too, was in the process of healing. We were two broken people who found joy when we were together.

The day Andy walked down my driveway and into my life, it had been over twenty years since we'd seen each other – and much longer since the first time he'd seen me. "Seen me" is the best way of putting it, since that very first time I didn't see him. I was busy being prom queen and he was a young, eighteen-year-old sailor home on his first leave. He'd heard there was a dance at the local high school and came to check it out. Later, he told me he took a seat in a dark corner and watched me exclusively all evening. We'd seen each other rarely in the years that followed, when we were married to others and raising our children. I knew him only as an acquaintance.

Fortunately for Andy, the day he showed up in my driveway all those years later, I was just taking a big vegetable lasagna from the oven. Of course I invited him to eat with me.

Andy swallowed a bite of lasagna as he recalled the first night he saw me. "Yes, I watched you all night when you were the prom queen. I thought to myself, *'The girl of my dreams. I've just seen the girl of my dreams.'"*

I admit I blushed. "Andy, I'm a long way from being that girl, not only years older, but sadder and wiser." Finishing our meal, we settled in the wicker rockers on the porch. Andy was thrilled to see the hummingbirds hover so close to us at the feeders.

He got a dreamy look. "I memorized you. You had that sparkly thing on your head."

I burst out in a hearty laugh. "It's called a tiara. You do have a good memory. I'd forgotten that." I was glad somebody remembered me twenty pounds ago.

He continued, "You wore a long, white gown and yellow roses on your shoulder. The roses were the same gold as your hair."

He had me reminiscing. "Yes, I borrowed my cousin's gorgeous white ball gown. Such a lovely dress: there were seed-pearls all down the front. I don't think they make them that fancy anymore."

I finally steered him away from discussing the prom. Frankly at this distance, I was slightly ashamed – prom queens, cheerleaders, and football jocks seemed kind of phony looking back.

We talked and talked that first night and discovered we had so much in common. He was the first male I'd ever met who loved reading as much as I did. We both shared regrets, he for guilt over not being more attentive and loving to his late wife, and my regrets over a failed marriage. Lost in conversation, we were surprised when we heard my clock boom out the midnight hour. We shared a discrete handshake as Andy got in his car and left.

The next day, I was surprised to see a flower truck drive up. I opened the box to bright yellow roses with a note, "Remember these? Just the color of your hair." I laughed in spite of myself. What a romantic!

Two years earlier I'd had a mastectomy. The day before surgery, a practitioner measured my breast for size, shape and weight. She told me there are eight different shapes of breasts. Who knew? She also told me a prosthesis of my exact breast would be ready after the incision healed. Up to now I'd thought "prosthesis" was an arm or leg, but evidently breasts could also be prosthetics. She was proved right. The prosthesis stuck in my left bra was not discernable from the right. In fact, it was ample. And I healed very quickly.

Now fully recovered, I remembered the warning from the doctors. The day after the surgery, I lay aching in my hospital bed, relieved the surgery was behind me so I could concentrate on healing. My surgeon entered the room accompanied by another doctor. He was introduced as a plastic surgeon. Together they urged me to have reconstructive surgery. I resisted, as I had already searched the pros and cons and chose not to pursue reconstructive surgery. After much persuasion from both of them, my surgeon took a deep breath and stated, "You're an attractive woman, but without this surgery no man will ever look at you again."

Shaking with anger, I snapped, "I wouldn't have any interest in a man so shallow that it would make a difference!" Those words were ringing in my memory when I realized Andy was romantically interested in me. I made him look at one side of my chest. I watched him closely. He didn't wince, squirm, or look uncomfortable.

He said, "I'm sorry you had to go through that." Then he gathered me in his arms tenderly. I felt cherished, so cherished. Then, that rascal got a twinkle in his eyes and said, "Now let me see the other one."

I gave him a hardy swat. "No way!"

When my sister Jennie perceived my interest in Andy, she asked, "Is it time to break out the chains?"

I said, "Meet Andy and if you think I need them, I'll cool it." But she loved him almost as much as I did. After all my determination to never marry again, and proving my breast surgeon wrong, we married a month later. I was sixty-three and Andy was sixty-seven.

Andy assumed I'd sell my house in New York State and we'd live in his house in Key West. I disagreed, "No way. I just paid off my mortgage, and all my children live here. Let's think of another way." Our compromise was to spend six months in Florida and six months in New York. That's how we ended up with two houses, not because we were rich, but because we were stubborn.

I remember the beginning of our marriage as days filled with light and love. The trip to Key West was magical. As we crossed the Seven Mile Bridge, the astonishing blue-green water was so clear we could see the neon fish through the depths. Flowers were blooming everywhere. Standing in front of our house and looking up the street, there was a tunnel of pure color in a canopy of flowers over the road. A lovely surprise for me, Andy had a yard full of banana trees in various stages of blossom and huge bunches of ripe bananas.

As one day bled into another, we lived in that paradise of flowers and banana trees. There were a few bumps along the road as I made it clear I was not joining the Garden Club or the Yacht Club or taking art lessons. In short, I was not wife number two, to be fitted into the pattern of wife number one like a missing piece to a puzzle. One day I walked into the kitchen and overheard Andy making arrangements for me to attend the Garden Club. "She'll be there," I heard him say, adding, "You'll love her."

"What was that about?" I asked.

He said, "Oh, I was just making sure of the time the Garden Club meets. They're expecting you at two tomorrow."

I was furious. I had retired from a job I loved at the Cornell Hotel School in Ithaca. The only part of my job I didn't love were the endless meetings I had to attend. With retirement I vowed to never set foot in a meeting again. "Andy, I'm not going to that meeting or any other meeting. I hate meetings, I hate clubs and I am not going to be fitted into the slot Milli filled. Understand that right now."

Andy looked puzzled and said, "But I told her you'd be there. Call and tell her you're not coming."

I said, "No, I'm not calling her and I'm not going. If I don't show up, she'll figure I'm not coming."

That was about as intense as a disagreement would get between the two of us.

One of the restaurants we loved was Blue Heaven, located in Bahama Village, a large courtyard in the seedier section of Key West. We drove there because nobody walked there after dark. The food was delicious: pork falling off the bone, fried plantains and rice with black beans. The ever-playing band performed as Banty chickens and brilliantly-feathered roosters strolled the flagstones, pecking at crumbs. Bright lights were strung in the trees and there was camaraderie among us as we mellowed on Sangria. Now and then a rooster would crow from a high branch of the overhanging trees. As the waitress walked to the cash register with our bill, Andy said, "Watch her face." A little jealous of her perfect figure in her skimpy shorts, I was glad he wanted to watch her face. Her face lit up with delight as she quickly returned to our table and gave Andy a big kiss on the cheek.

"What was that all about?" I asked.

Andy chuckled, "Remember, I always say, 'Whatever is worth doing is worth doing in excess.'"

Still puzzled, I asked, "What does that have to do with your kiss?"

"I gave her a $50 tip," he answered.

## FINDING FAITH

One day, as I was busy with kitchen chores, Andy came in from trimming his banana trees. I'm always singing or whistling as second nature; sometimes I don't even realize I'm doing it. So when Andy walked in, I was singing loudly, "Yes, I belong to Jesus and He belongs to me. Not for the years of life alone, but for eternity." Andy looked at me and said, "Do you really believe that? Can we be positive we really belong to Jesus? Sometimes I think I do. Then other times I doubt I'm even saved. I wish I had your certainty."

I stopped wiping the counter and said, "Of course you can be certain. The great thing about the Bible is that it's very profound and yet very simple."

Andy washed the banana tree sap from his hands and said, "I wish I was as sure as you are."

I looked at him seriously. "Are you kidding? The Bible is so clear on this, there is absolutely no guessing. Here, I'll show you." I grabbed my Bible from the stool where I'd laid it and flipped to the book of Romans. "Here, it's as plain as plain can be. 'For if you tell others with your own mouth that Jesus Christ is your Lord and believe in your own heart that God has raised him from the dead, you will be saved.'" *(Romans 10:9)*. I handed him the Bible, "Here Andy, read it for yourself."

Andy prayed, "Yes, Lord, I do believe Christ rose from the dead. Remove my doubts." Then Andy raised his head and said, "But I don't feel any different."

I answered, "Where does it talk about feelings in this verse? Unless God is a liar you are saved whether you feel like it or not."

We often watched a local Key West pastor, Morris Wright, on TV. Andy said, "Now there's a pastor I could relate to."

I took him up on it, "Why not?" We began attending his church. He and Andy were made for each other. Pastor Wright combined Bible truth with a sense of humor similar to Andy's. He often ministered to the many homeless in Key West where they congregated under the bridges. Some lived in discarded refrigerator cardboard boxes, others just strung up a tarp to keep out the rain. Armed with a box of doughnuts or hamburgers, Pastor Wright visited them. Many then came to church and, more importantly, came to Christ.

Pastor Wright's sermons were spiked with humor and Andy often laughed so vigorously that our long wooden pew shook. Along with the humor, we were learning significant Bible truths. He confirmed to Andy that feelings had nothing do with the truth of Christ's salvation. He emphasized, "For by grace are ye saved through faith; and that not of yourselves: it is the gift of God: Not of works, lest any man should boast." (*Ephesians 2:8-9, KJV*). In essence the sermons were like Jesus Himself stepped out of the Bible pages and loved us. We experienced such calm, peace, and, yes, joy.

During all these first few years, there was never any indication my husband's sharp mind was failing in any way. He oversaw taxes, checkbooks, tree fertilizer schedules, and car maintenance effortlessly. Most importantly, I felt dearly loved and deeply cherished. I returned the love and sought to make him feel equally cherished.

## KEEPING TIME

Twelve years later, I was seeing the first warning signs that my beloved was disappearing. He was still a delightful companion, loving and thoughtful, but there was a subtle daily slippage.

One of the signs of Alzheimer's is a short attention span. For about the fifth time in the last hour, Andy asked, "What time is it?" Not realizing I was inflicting a cruelty, I replied, "Just look at the clock," as I pointed to the clock on the wall.

He looked puzzled and said, "I don't know what that machine means." Not only was he unable to tell time, he'd forgotten what a clock was.

A horror of sadness washed over me anew as I observed another slippage of his brilliant mind. I turned my face away as the unbidden tears washed down my face. Giving him a fierce hug, I said, "Darling, it's 2 o'clock.

Why don't you take a nap?" Settled into bed with a warm afghan, he was soon asleep.

I was almost paralyzed with fear. I was watching a person slowly disappear while his body was still functioning. I sat at the kitchen table and let the weeping I'd held at bay in his presence overtake me. After the sodden, fruitless cry, I implored, "Lord, give me a sign you are in this with me. Give me a sign that I can weather this storm. I know only doubters ask for a sign, but I need a sign from you that you are in this sad journey with me. I know that only doubters ask for a sign, but at this sad juncture I'm a doubter. I'm doubting I can live through the slow death of a brilliant brain. Doubting I can withstand the dismal outlook for the future, even doubting your presence, Lord. I'm asking for a sure sign that you're in this with me."

Drying my tears and reapplying my lipstick, I realized I'd better make a quick trip to Walmart for last minute Christmas goodies. Making a mental note to look for Andy's cider, I headed out.

I pushed my cart through the aisles noting the high spirits and joyful attitudes of the other shoppers on this day before Christmas. They were consulting their shopping lists and pondering the best surprises for their loved ones. Then I noticed, near the bakery, a shopper sitting in a wheelchair. She looked perky despite her obvious disability, a jaunty red ribbon tying back her hair. I thought, *She's making the best of a bad situation*, as she smiled broadly at me. A short little woman, I had to bend down to speak to her. We chatted briefly. She told me she was waiting for her daughter who was finishing her shopping. I admired her large-faced watch. "I've been looking for a watch like that with a large face. Where did you get it?"

Quick as a wink she grabbed my hand and put the watch on my wrist. "Here, I want you to have it," she told me. I protested, after all you don't take a watch from an obviously impoverished little old lady. She shook her head and her blue eyes sparkled as she replied, "This is meant for you. This morning I prayed with my daughter that I could give a gift to someone today. For the first time in my life I have no money to buy gifts and no one special in mind. We prayed for the Lord to lead us to a needy person for me to give a gift to. I have nothing, so I felt it was a fruitless prayer. When I saw you push your cart up the aisle, the Lord said to me—'that's the person.' When you came up to me, it was a confirmation. When you admired my watch, I knew this was the gift I had to give."

I was in awe. I silently asked, *Lord, is this the sign of your presence I was seeking? Is this the sign that you are in this nightmare of Alzheimer's with me?*

Just then her daughter arrived, cheery and pushing a cart of plastic-bagged purchases. I turned to her and showed her the watch her mother gave me, now on my arm. I said, "Your mother just gave this to me, is that all right?"

She was exuberant, "Oh yes! We prayed together this morning that Mom could give a gift to someone today and this is the answer to our prayer. Praise God! You are an answer to our prayer." With that they both beamed at me and left the store.

I realized the Lord had also answered *my* prayer. I had the watch to prove it. Standing in that Walmart bakery, joy washed over me. Sheer joy. I realized all the circumstances the Lord had used to bring me this sign that He indeed is watching over me—even in Alzheimer's. I was reminded of this promise from scripture: "The joy of the Lord is your strength." *(Nehemiah 8:10).*

# Chapter Three

# Key West

Key West was the perfect setting for our first months of marriage. Actually, we enjoyed several months of honeymoon. We were both walkers, and we walked daily over the whole island. One of our favorite walks was a few blocks from our home over the bridge to Houseboat Row.

Here along the ocean's edge were several brilliantly-painted houseboats. Whimsical and varying in size from small houses to simply decks with lounge chairs, they were anchored near a high concrete embankment. Most were anchored in from cold northern ports to spend the winter months in sunny Key West, where temperatures ranged from 80° to 95° all winter. There were colorful boats with flower boxes overflowing in a profusion of brilliant blooms spilling over the sides. Key West offered an endless summer, where limes grew wild for the picking and avocados grew too huge for our neighbors to sell commercially. Several of the houseboats had gardens planted in 10-gallon pails. One especially noticeable had a variety of tomatoes on a sunny deck, from huge beefsteak gems to tiny cherry tomatoes and lots of green ones ripening in the sun. Looking closely, we discovered an array of every type of vegetable growing in pots and pails. One houseboat even displayed a decorative cotton plant swaying in the breeze.

About midway up the long row, we were greeted by a young bearded hippie-type in cutoff jeans with a wild mat of glistening chest hair. He was seated at a makeshift table with a huge wheel of cheese taking up most of the table. "Hey, I'm Brad," he introduced himself. "Want some Wisconsin cheese?" He indicated some overturned pails where we could sit down and join him. Brad sliced off hunks of cheese with his jackknife and told us he'd arrived only yesterday. We eyed his boat, astounded.

"You traveled all that way in your boat?" Andy asked.

Laughing heartily as he brushed wild black curls from his eyes he said, "Oh no. I came here with my car transport truck. I store my houseboat on Stock Island and pick it up every November, live in it until April, then store it again."

By now our curiosity knew no bounds. I asked, "A car transport truck? Explain."

"Lots of my neighbors in Madison winter here in Key West; most of them in the over-seventy crowd," he explained. "They love it here, but not the thousand-mile trip by car. I bring the cars down on my transport truck and they fly down. Their cars are here when they arrive."

Satisfied with this explanation, Andy asked, "How is living six months on a houseboat?"

Brad took another swipe at his stubborn locks. I noticed his eyes were the same color as the ocean behind him. He answered enthusiastically, "Oh, I love it! The ocean waves rock the boat just like a rocking chair. Going to sleep in a gently rocking boat is sublime. It's very economical too. No taxes, no electric bills. I run off a generator. It's the perfect life for a vagabond like me."

Andy and I were eating alternately huge slabs and tiny curls of delicious cheese. Andy gave a critical look over at the boat. "How do you anchor it, Brad? It doesn't look very secure. Don't you bang against the concrete?"

Brad cut off another piece of cheese, grabbed a cracker, and stuck both in his mouth, biting into them before he answered. "Oh, the ocean's so calm, all I need is my anchor."

Andy disagreed. "You should have it firmly-anchored in place. A few big waves could bang your boat to pieces."

Brad was peacefully chewing and gave a dismissive nod. "Oh no, it's always calm in here."

Andy rose up to leave, "This could be habit-forming," he said. "We'd better start walking or we'll decide to join you on your boat."

A short half-block walk from the houseboats was Martha's, our favorite restaurant that served fresh seafood. We never really got to try much seafood because we were addicted to the Rock Lobster. We feasted on huge local lobster, bigger than a fist, served on its own platter with a bowl of clarified butter and crusty bread. This was our frequent favorite indulgence. There were big windows overlooking the ocean where we often watched flickering lights of passing boats in the darkness as we dined.

Another of our favorite walks was to Hemingway House. Almost a museum, there was a slight charge to enter the former home of early 20th century novelist Ernest Hemingway. The estate was surrounded by a high stone wall. Inside the gate, dozens of cats strolled and lounged throughout the grounds. Most of the cats were polydactyl. Some had so many toes, their feet looked like powder puffs. Inside, the house was much the same as Hemingway left it, with all the furnishings intact. I imagined I could smell cigar smoke in his bedroom, which featured a catwalk to his treehouse writing studio. We were told he often rose from bed, took the catwalk to the studio, and wrote in the early morning hours.

At the time of our visit, it had *literally* become a catwalk. We watched as cats nimbly navigated the distance from bedroom to studio. Some cats were stretched out for naps on the ledges of the studio. There was no doubt cats reigned at Hemingway House. Attendants put out cardboard boxes for the cats to shelter them from the wind on stormy days.

Andy loved our visits to Hemingway House especially because he loved cats. Near the pool, Andy pointed out an odd receptacle. "See that? It's a urinal Hemingway carried over on his back from Sloppy Joe's."

"Andy, I know you're making that up," I challenged.

Laughing, he replied, "No, it's documented truth. He was drinking at Sloppy Joe's when they remodeled the men's room. They were about to discard the urinal when he picked it up on his shoulders and brought it here. It's been here ever since. It was incorporated into the pool."

Sloppy Joe's is a nearby saloon that Hemingway frequented as his favorite drinking hole. A distinction of Sloppy Joe's is the ceiling hung with women's bras. Even today you are invited to hang your bra from the ceiling, a dubious honor I chose to bypass.

Andy pointed out the penny embedded in the concrete near the pool and told me, "Hemingway tossed it there when he found out the pool cost $20,000. He told his wife, 'Here, take my last penny.' Then he made sure it became part of the pool."

Andy and I sat on a bench in the sun to watch the parade of cats.

"Look," Andy exclaimed. "I think that fellow has the hugest feet of all." The tiger cat walking near had feet almost as big as saucers. We burst out laughing as he strutted by.

It wasn't unusual for cats to jump up on Andy's lap. Whenever we went visiting, the family cat strolled in and soon hopped up on Andy's lap. It became our private joke to see how long it took before he was petting a cat on his lap.

Another quirky tradition in Key West is the daily celebration of the sunset. This takes place at Sunset Pier, where you can watch as the sun sinks into the ocean. Anyone with an act is welcome to show up and perform. We loved the holiday atmosphere and watching the various performers. I was most baffled by the man who stood on a platform about 12 feet off the ground and lifted a heavy iron kitchen stove high in the air with just his teeth. After the show, I sneaked over and tested to see if the stove was really lightweight plastic. No, I couldn't budge the heavy metal stove. There were also silver-painted "statues" who stood motionless for hours with free-will offering vases near their feet. Andy never passed them without a generous offering.

But his favorite act was the Cat Man. The Cat Man had several cats that performed nightly. Some jumped through a flaming hoop with apparent ease, others walked a tightrope without falling. Andy and I were amazed anew each time we watched the Cat Man. We often stayed after their acts because Andy liked to help put the cats back in their cages for the ride home. One night, I sat and waited until Andy returned, telling me excitedly, "You wouldn't believe how obedient those cats are to his every word. They all ride home in cages except for one that rides on his shoulder."

I was equally impressed. "Does he train them from kittens? How do you get a cat to obey?"

Andy said, "No, these are just wandering alley cats he picks up," Andy said. "They're not hand-raised. Just imagine training a cat to obey anything. It's just amazing!"

## A STORMY NIGHT

Half a block from our house was a great Cuban restaurant we loved called the Red Pig. There was a big statue of a pig out front, appropriately painted bright red. It was so large, children often climbed on and pretended they were riding a pony. We enjoyed a meal of rice and black beans, fried plantains, and a rich flan for dessert, washed down with their homemade Sangria. Totally sated, we went to sleep on a waterbed in our peaceful treehouse bedroom.

I was awakened by a ferocious wind whipping the banana trees outside the balcony. Andy stood at the open doors of our balcony. "This wind is tremendous. It has shredded all the leaves on the banana trees, they're just threads flapping in the wind." He closed the doors to the balcony and began getting dressed.

I rose up from my warm cocoon. "Surely you don't plan to go out in this storm?"

"I wouldn't dream of it ordinarily, but Brad didn't have that boat secured nearly tight enough. He'll be up trying to secure it in this storm. If it's bad here, it's ten times worse at the ocean. Go back to sleep, there's nothing you can do," Andy said, pulling on his pants. I was already scrambling out of bed. I pulled on long pants, the first I'd been out of shorts since landing at Key West.

Andy gave a long sigh of resignation; he already knew if I made up my mind to do something, there was no changing it. "Get a warm jacket," he told me, "preferably with a hood."

Bundled against the wind, we started the two-block walk to Houseboat Row. Near the bridge, we passed a little dump loaded with discarded tires. Andy sorted through them, handing one to me and carrying one in each hand as we continued. We walked bent against the wind, howling so fiercely I could barely hear as Andy shouted, "I knew Brad didn't have that thing anchored properly. He needs these tires between him and the concrete wall."

Sure enough, when we arrived, Brad was frantically trying to stop the boat from hitting against the wall. The ocean waves were so high, they washed over the sidewalk. Fortunately, bright streetlights illuminated his efforts. We could see he wasn't having much luck as the boat kept banging over and over against the wall.

Andy had a coil of sturdy rope in each pocket. Still holding the tires, he managed to climb on board the pitching boat and started unreeling the rope. Soon, he had a rope attached to one of the tires, which he tied to the boat, then secured to the heavy iron railing above the concrete. In minutes, he had the other tire placed as a buffer between the boat and concrete wall. He motioned me to come aboard with the third tire. "No way!" Balancing between a madly pitching boat and the wave-drenched sidewalk in a raging storm? No way! I couldn't even swim. As if this would have made any difference in this tempest.

Giving up on me, Andy came ashore to get the third tire. We stood on the sidewalk awash by the ocean waves, both of us drenched. Suddenly, Andy grabbed me in a fierce hug. After a long, lingering kiss in the midst of all that turbulence, I shouted, "This isn't the time or place for kissing."

He shouted above the din, "It's always time for romance!"

I laughed despite myself as Andy grabbed the third tire and swung back onto the boat. Standing there in that battering storm, I felt so loved, so cherished. In these wild, crazy circumstances, Andy took time, as he put it, "for romance."

Andy put the third tire in place and the boat at last had a buffer between boat and concrete wall. Now the boat was pushing harmlessly against the tires. Finally Andy was satisfied that Brad was safe in the storm and we returned home. After hot coffee and buttery toast, we fell into bed and slept till noon.

We woke up to bright sunshine. The only reminders of the vicious storm were the shredded banana leaves. Andy looked over at me. "Let's go on a picnic today. We need to do something fun after that harrowing night."

I quickly agreed. "I'll fix sandwiches and throw together a few things."

Andy laid a restraining hand on me. "No, I'll furnish the food. You just relax."

I snorted. "Andy, we both know you can't cook."

He agreed. "Who said anything about cooking? I said I'll furnish the picnic. Not cook, furnish."

Doubtful, I agreed. I tried to stay out of the room as he fussed with the picnic basket and what I only hoped would be lunch.

In the car, driving with the sparkling blue water on each side of the road, I asked where we were headed. Hands on the wheel, his hat tilted at a rakish angle, he answered, "Just up the road a little way. Bahia Honda is a small state park with lots of birds. Manatees come there to drink fresh water and, best of all, we can wade far out into the Atlantic in shallow water."

Andy's promise proved true. We wandered far into the ocean on the sandy bottom. The waves swirled slowly around my knees. The quiet, peacefulness and utter calm were so welcome after the turbulent night before. The only sound was the singing of the birds and the gentle lap of waves on shore. I consciously imprinted this peace deep within my soul as my place to go to during times of duress. It proved reliable: sitting in the dentist's chair during a root canal, during colonoscopies and other dreaded necessary nastinesses of life, I often escaped mentally to that wonderful, peaceful walk in the ocean.

Back in the park, I sat at a table near the ocean while Andy got the picnic basket. I was curious about the meal he'd provide. It proved to be the perfect picnic. He pulled out a big, green avocado and expertly sliced it in half, removed the pit, opened a can of sardines and produced a salt shaker. I'd noticed he'd grabbed a lime from our tree as we got in the car. He cut the lime in half, squeezed some on each avocado, sprinkled it liberally with salt, and then he dumped half the sardines into each avocado. He tore off a generous hunk of Cuban bread and we had the perfect meal. It was the perfect picnic. That proved to be the combination for all of our future picnics.

We strolled near the docks and watched as a manatee sucked water from a fresh water hose. Andy showed me the long, abandoned Bahia Honda Rail Bridge standing now as just a skeleton – a skeleton alive with birds and nests built in every crevice. We sat on the sand and watched as several ospreys flew in with fish dangling from their beaks to feed their young. There was such a clamor as the tiny beaks strained for the fish. Andy cocked his head to one side and said, "Listen – I hear them saying, 'Feed me, feed me, feed me first, Mommy.'" I listened carefully, and he was right, you could hear the baby birds begging for food.

We drove home with the setting sun staining the water on each side of the highway with a bright crimson glow.

We were "like them that dream." That period was a time when God showered on us, "above what we asked or even dreamed of." Aside from our deep love for each other, we were experiencing being known and loved by our beloved Creator. The Lord loaded us daily with answers to prayer and opened the scriptures to us with new and deep insights into the Word. We were being healed; Andy from the searing grief of losing his first wife, Milli, and I, suffering from the cruelty and ravages of a failed marriage.

The truth is, we were growing in the Lord and healing: "It was like a dream. How we laughed and sang for joy. What amazing things the Lord has done for us. Yes, glorious things. What wonder, what joy!" *(Psalm 126:1-3)*. It *was* as though we were living in a dream; that was the reality of our lives at that time.

Blissfully, we had no inkling of Alzheimer's or the sad things to come. In fact, probably neither of us had ever heard the word. Alzheimer's disease is usually a complete surprise to its victims and their families. No one expects it. The terrible separation it would bring to our lives and relationship were undreamed of.

I couldn't have imagined the day would come when this dearly-loved companion would look at me blankly and ask, "Who are you?" I couldn't foresee this brilliant Certified Public Accountant would one day be unable to balance a simple checkbook. Nor could I imagine my suave, handsome husband could be reduced to a petulant four-year-old, throwing a tantrum to get his own way.

The Lord speaks of the "Land of Forgetfulness" is Psalm 88:12. Later in that Psalm, a sad, but true commentary, "Lover, friend, acquaintance — all gone." *(Psalm, 88:18)*.

Yet, even in this deep, hopeless valley, the Lord extends comfort. I found comfort in the wonderful revelation of the Lord from the book of Malachi, where we're told God has a diary where our names are written. Think of it! In the rare instance of our names appearing in someone's diary, it's usually in a love relationship. No less a love relationship when we're told: "Then those who feared and loved the Lord spoke often of Him to each other. And He had a Book of Remembrance (diary) drawn up in which He recorded the names of those who feared Him and loved to think about Him." *(Malachi 3:16)*.

On this frightening road of Alzheimer's, I have the comfort of knowing that the Lord is watching. "Like a refiner of silver, He will sit and closely watch…so they will do their work for God with pure hearts." *(Malachi 3:3)*.

I also had the promise: "Now glory be to God who by his mighty power at work within us is able to do far more than we would ever dare to ask or even dream of — infinitely beyond our highest prayers, desires, thoughts, or hopes." *(Ephesians 3:20)*.

# Chapter Four

## Rage

Lately Andy seemed to be in a continuous simmering rage about to explode. And explode, he did, at unexpected times. When it happened, all blame and exasperation rested solely on me.

A repairman named Jeff was coming out to check a leak around our bathroom window. I mentioned it to Andy as we drank our six o'clock coffee: "Jeff will be out around ten. Let's be dressed and showered when he gets here."

Andy's response was an unexpected explosion! "Do you think you have to boss my every move? Of course I'll be dressed, do you think I'm a slobbering fool?"

At eight, showered and dressed after breakfast, Andy took up a watch by the front window. He repeatedly asked what time Jeff was arriving and I repeatedly answered, "After ten." Andy continued his vigil at the window.

He met Jeff at the door, accompanying him throughout the inspection. He asked Jeff several times if he knew what he was doing – to the point of embarrassment. He stayed on the back porch as Jeff was leaving. I attempted an apology as he climbed into his truck, but Jeff stopped me. "Don't give it another thought. My Dad had Alzheimer's. I recognized it the minute he first greeted me."

Andy joined me as Jeff's pickup left the driveway. I glanced at him and was surprised at his red face. He was trembling and literally shaking with rage. "You bitch, you goddamned bitch. Why did you let me stand here for hours watching for him when you knew right along when he was coming? You goddamned bitch, no wonder I hate you." Over and over, "Why didn't you tell me?"

No point in arguing, he obsessed for over an hour. I silently told myself, *This is not the real Andy. This is not my beloved.* The real Andy was endlessly loving and kind. I recalled an incident when we were newly married, about fifteen years ago. I was the one in an angry snit. The issue was so minute, I can no longer remember the source of my angry outburst. As I was listing my grievances, Andy had just looked at me with love and a slight smile. When I slowed down in my list of incriminations he noted, "Do you realize how beautiful you are when you're all fired up? Your eyes sparkle, your face is flushed so rosy, and you are even more gorgeous."

"Andy, pay attention to what I'm saying."

He replied, "I will later, but right now just let me enjoy this new aspect of you. I've never seen you so animated." I sputtered a few times, then could no longer hold in a hearty laugh. "You rascal!" We both ended up laughing till the tears rolled down our cheeks.

Now, faced with his explosive rage, I tried to recall the real Andy. "Let's go out on the porch and have a cup of coffee. You must be starved."

Was I sick of being blamed? Exceedingly! In the past, before Alzheimer's, I'd observed that other women caregivers whose husbands suffered with dementia had a tension, worried eyes and looked stressed. Now I knew why. Now it was me. I wore tension like a cloak. It was not so much about what was happening to my dear, loved companion right then, but the fear of what might happen tomorrow, next week, next month. When I tried to think ahead even to the next year, I couldn't go there. He was already so remote from the real Andy – he was truly not the same person.

I'd spent the day with a four-year-old. An early morning tantrum, mumbling and cursing under his breath, that ended with a blinding rage as he threw his wallet across the room. It bounced off the wall and landed at my feet. "You goddamned bitch. You asked Walter's advice about the leaky tire, why didn't you ask me? Why didn't you ask one of my kids? Do you think me and my kids are too dumb to know how to fix a leaky tire?"

"Andy, I did ask you and you shrugged and told me to 'take care of it and not bother you', so I asked Walter." This was followed by a half-day pout, contrary to what Dr. P told me when he had said, "I love Alzheimer's patients because they can't remember long enough to carry a grudge."

And it was strange. At most I would see a twenty-minute retention, hence the "What day is it, what time is it, where are we?" But on that day it had been over three hours that the grievance had been hashed over, raged over, and repeated endlessly, "Do you think me and my kids are too dumb to know about leaky tires?" To my credit, I didn't rise to the bait – this time.

At the monthly caregiver's group, I discovered others were being similarly cursed. The men especially distressed that their formerly loving wives even knew such words. One man declared, "In over twenty years of marriage I never once heard her curse. Now, it's every day. And always aimed at me." As a group, we all agreed it was best to ignore the cursing and not lecture or make a big issue of the cursing. Changing the subject seemed to be the best coping measure.

The tricky part was never knowing what would trigger an explosion. On a quiet Sunday morning, we'd finished drinking our coffee on the porch, overlooking the view of Cornell and Ithaca. It was so quiet and peaceful I could discern the individual bird calls. The cat jumped up on Andy's lap, totally ignoring the squirrels at the birdfeeder. I left Andy and the cat drowsing in the sun to dress for church.

I put on the last of my makeup and was trying to decide on earrings when Andy suddenly burst into the bedroom screaming, "You goddamn bitch! You are worthless to me. I've lost my wallet and you don't even care. My credit card, license and Social Security cards are all in it, and you don't even care. Just go off with your friends and leave me here still hunting."

By now, losing his wallet was a daily affair. That, and losing his glasses became a daily hunt. The daily hunt was, in fact, so daily, I'd gone to the Dollar Store and bought three wallets that resembled his close enough. I removed some of his current credit cards and replaced them with expired ones and various AARP cards and three one-dollar bills in each one. I also bought extra pairs of glasses, thus saving hours of hunting and frustration.

This time, the outburst only worsened after he found his wallet. "It was in my handkerchief drawer and you didn't even help me look for it," he yelled. "You goddamned bitch, you just don't care." He wasn't just angry, he was furious! I didn't comment, just inserted my earrings and pushed back my bangs. Maybe that's what infuriated him.

I repeated to myself, *I'm dealing with a four-year old, I'm dealing with a four-year old. Give me patience, Lord.* Although some part of me knew some four-year olds can at least be reasoned with.

At church, I noted what I felt was a personal message to me: "The Lord isn't too weak to save you ...He can hear you when you call." *(Isaiah 59:1).* How many times I'd cried silently, *Oh Lord, help me. Please help me to be patient, loving, and respectful to the person Andy really is, not this stranger in his place.* What a comfort to know He does hear when I call.

## CONFUSION

Andy loved watching the Olympics, especially the downhill skiing. We both watched with avid interest. It was such a normal, everyday event, both of us interested in the same thing. Peace settled around me. Maybe Andy wasn't so far from reality as I'd feared. He knew all the parameters of the sport, the names of all the major competitors and was watching, animated by the action and the thrill of speed. We sat cheering the Americans and Finnish athletes equally when they won the gold. Suddenly, Andy turned to me, "I'm so proud of you."

Puzzled, I asked, "Why?"

He was so animated and replied enthusiastically, "The way you skied down that hill yesterday and took the gold medal. Of course I'm proud of you. You did great!"

Peace left me and a cold chill replaced it. He'd identified me with Lindsey Vonn, who'd taken a gold medal a few minutes ago. We weren't on the same page at all. I remembered what Dr. P told me—never argue. "Oh, that," I replied. "Let's just watch and see what's next."

Hours later, I was sound asleep. It was 3 a.m. and my foot was being grasped and jiggled. Groggy, I opened my eyes to find Andy at the foot of the bed, staring at me, his eyes wild and full of fear. "How can you just lie there and sleep while they are out there stealing us blind? Get up and help me drive them out!" Still half asleep, I begged, "Go back to sleep, you're having a bad dream." He grew increasingly angry and shook my leg violently and screamed, "It's no dream! GET UP and HELP ME!" I reluctantly left my warm cocoon and followed as he rammed out of the bedroom and ran wildly through the whole house. "Damn them! They left as soon as you got up."

Finally, at 4 a.m., I had him settled into bed after a hot cup of chamomile tea. I placed his oxygen nodules firmly in his nose and made sure the machine was turned on, as he often got up in the night and turned it off. He was sound asleep and snoring in just minutes. I never did get back to sleep. Poor, poor me.

Another day, I returned home from church and Andy suggested we take a walk. I laced up my sneakers and started out the door. Andy put out a restraining hand on me. "Let's wait for the other one. We shouldn't leave her here all alone."

The familiar cold chill passed over me, "What other one? There's only you and me here."

He looked so puzzled and hurt. "What about my sister, Lilli? I've been talking to her all morning, while you were in church. We can't just leave her here all alone."

Throwing aside gentleness, goodness and understanding, I blurted, "Andy, she's been dead for twenty years. I'm the only one here. The only one who's been here all day."

Looking very confused, Andy replied, "You mean I thought you were my sister Lilli all day? I must really be wacko."

And with that, we were on a different plateau, the first time he'd mistaken me for someone else. Thankfully, he wouldn't feel bad about it for long. By the time we returned from our short walk, his sister Lilli was forgotten; or maybe I was her.

We sat on the back porch drinking coffee and watching the cardinals in the Palmetto bushes when Andy leaned over and whispered, "You know, this facility is really in bad shape. I've noticed the electric plugs are not screwed in tight, insulation is falling out and all the doors are half off their hinges. Even all the faucets drip continually. Nothing in this facility is up to par, but I guess we have to stay here and keep our mouths shut."

I came up with my pat answer that always satisfied him. "You know, I think you're right." But I couldn't help but wonder where the descriptions originated. Ours was a newly-built house, not yet old enough for drippy faucets or unhinged doors.

One of our last shared pleasures was driving around the countryside on random excursions with no real destination. We both thrilled to the unexpected deer encounter or flock of wild turkeys. One such leisurely drive was interrupted with sudden loud screaming, "Stop the car! Stop the car!" Andy opened the door while the car was still moving and flung himself out. He stumbled, fell, then caught his balance. Quickly turning off the ignition, I raced back to him. "What's the matter, what happened?"

"You were going the wrong way. Nothing was familiar, we'll never get to the North Van Etten Cemetery going this way. You were going in the wrong direction!"

He was frantic and wild-eyed. I laid a hand on his shoulder. "You're right. Get in and I'll go in the other direction." Saddened, I had to admit to myself it was no longer safe to take him driving. The enormous damage that could happen if he jumped out at even 20 miles an hour could be devastating. One more door of the things we could do together slammed shut.

I was often asked by friends who knew the 'Real Andy,' "Aren't you angry he's been taken away from you?" I thought about this as I drove slowly home. *No, I'm not angry, but very, very frightened. So afraid of what's next, what fresh horror awaits us?*

I remembered a promise the Lord had given me, "For I know the plans I have for you, says the Lord. They are plans for good and not for evil, to give you a future and a hope." *(Jeremiah 29:11)*.

*Yes, Lord, I desperately need a future hope.*

# Chapter Five

# Wandering

I still didn't realize Andy couldn't be left alone. I came home from water aerobics one morning and found him walking along the road, exhausted in the 80° heat and leaning on his walking stick. I stopped and, as he got in the car, his forehead dripping sweat, he exclaimed, "Thank God you came along. I'm so tired I could never have made it home."

"Where were you? You told me you planned to spend the morning on the porch chasing the squirrels away from the birdfeeders."

Exasperated with me, he shouted, "I was at the cemetery. I was looking for my Dad and my brother Emil's graves. I walked and walked; I searched all over, but couldn't find them. Will you go back with me tomorrow and help me find them?" I realized he thought the Green Pine Cemetery in Florida was the one near our home in New York. Another sad wake-up call for me, he couldn't be left alone or he'd wander off. The Green Pine cemetery was two miles away, a four-mile trip both ways. No wonder he was exhausted.

"Yes, I'll help you find them tomorrow," I answered. "Let's go home now and drink some water and cool off." I needed to cool off, too.

## THE MIDDLE OF THE NIGHT

Because Andy sometimes got up in the middle of the night and thought it was daytime, I had to be alert even while sleeping. At 3 a.m. one morning, I woke up abruptly. Did I hear a noise? I looked over at Andy's bed. Empty! I went quickly from relaxed and sleepy to rigid alarm. I could vaguely hear rain. I glanced out into the pitch-dark night and saw it was pouring heavily. I slipped on my shoes and went to the other two bedrooms on the other side of the house. Sometimes Andy went to another bed if he was restless. No Andy. Growing more frantic by the minute, I went to the window again. There he was, standing in the very middle of the road, barely visible in the downpour. Not even grabbing a robe, I rushed out and screamed, "What are you doing?"

Rain dripped from his clothes and face. "I just came out to check if the garage is locked. I can't find the garage. Help me find the garage. I don't think I locked it last night. It's so dark, I can't find it. Help me find it." Now he was the frantic one. At our New York home, he was obsessive about locking our big storage garage every night. Now in the middle of the night, in the middle of a wild storm on a busy road in Florida, he was standing in drenched dark clothing. We were both frightened for different reasons.

"Come in the house," I pleaded. He obstinately refused to budge. "I'm not going in until I'm sure the garage is locked." I remembered Dr. P's warning to "Never argue with an Alzheimer's patient, you'll never win. Distraction is the only way to persuade."

Growing more frantic by the minute, I gently took Andy's arm. "Let's go get a flashlight and we can find it then." Finally, after an agonizing 20 minutes in the rain, in the middle of the road, he reluctantly came in. Fortunately the 20-minute attention span worked to my advantage and I got him dried and back into bed. It was 4 a.m. Within minutes, he was asleep. I never did get back to sleep. Too much adrenaline. I sat at the kitchen table and rested my head in my still-trembling hands. "Lord, you promised you'd never give us more than we can stand. Where is the escape in this situation?"

When I complained to my daughter, Cheryl, about Andy's midnight wanderings, she came up with a partial solution. Urging us to take a walk, she took advantage of our absence to install a deadbolt lock high up on the door. Instead of silently leaving in the middle of the night, Andy was stopped at the door. Now his leaving was done with much muttering and shaking of the door, enough to wake me up. I considered this a successful deterrent. A chain devise lock my son, Walter, installed in Florida, similarly helped. Upon our arrival in Florida, Andy immediately noticed the lock devise and commented, "Oh good, another line of defense against intruders." He never realized it was to keep him in rather than intruders out. Even though he knew it was there, it usually created enough of a deterrent that it woke me up when he decided to walk in the middle of the night.

There are bracelets especially designed to track the elderly prone to wandering. At the doctor's office, a man proudly showed us his bracelet. "See? It's a great devise. Now I can't get lost. There's a built-in tracking devise that shows wherever I'm at," he explained. Later in the car, Andy sputtered and fumed. "Just like a dog collar! Don't ever put a dog collar like that on me. Just like a run-away dog." His attitude was totally dismissive.

## A FATEFUL STOPOVER

Many years before Alzheimer's, we would make an annual trek from Key West to our home in Newfield, New York, where we spent summers. It was such a contrast from our tiny Key West yard to our spacious thirty acres of forest. This meant a huge garden and lots of roaming space. On the drive north, we always made a few days stopover in Fernandina Beach. We enjoyed walks on the beach and exploring the quaint historic town. But one year it rained and rained and rained, meaning no beach walks. Andy picked up a real estate brochure in the hotel lobby. Lounging on the bed, he suddenly sat bolt upright. "Listen to this! It sounds too good to be true."

He had my interest as he read, "Three bedroom, two bath, 12 foot-ceilings, double garage, and here's the best part, a one-acre yard." Our Key West yard was barely the size of a postage stamp. To us, a one-acre yard sounded sumptuous. Andy had such excitement in his voice. "Let's call the real estate number and find out where it is and go take a look."

The real estate agent did better than give us directions, she picked us up and drove us. While waiting for her, I remembered how quickly an argument could escalate. I said to Andy, "Let's have it firmly understood if either of us doesn't like it we are not going to wrangle and argue about it the rest of the trip. We are just looking, and we both agree or we both totally forget it."

Andy chuckled. "Agreed."

When we walked in the front door, the view from the huge living room looked out on a big expanse of lawn surrounded by a forest of tall pine trees. Andy grabbed my hand and whispered, "I love it." So did I. After touring the rest of the house, we were in love—spacious walk-in closets, spectacular bedroom with bay windows, and a bathroom almost as large as our *bedroom* in Key West.

We were both so positive this was "home" that Andy told the Realtor, "We want to make an offer."

Unbelievably, she objected. "I never let people buy the first house they see. Let's look around and see if you still want to make an offer." She took us to three more houses.

Andy was impatient, "Take us back to that first one." During our second tour, we loved the house even more. It was new construction and we discovered it had been the builder's model. It was also our heart's model. From the real estate office in Fernandina Beach, we listed the Key West house with a real estate friend.

Then we prayed and put out a fleece to the Lord. "If the Key West house sells within three months, we will consider this is in Your will. If it doesn't, we'll forget the Fernandina house." With that resolve, we continued our trip north.

When we walked in the door of our New York home two days later, the phone was ringing. The house in Key West had a committed buyer. Just that quick, we went from the farthermost southern spot in Florida to the farthermost northern spot in Florida. We located just eight miles south of the Georgia border and ten miles north of Jacksonville. All the mechanics of moving went smoothly. We were in such joy in our new spacious home. Walter drove the moving van from Key West to Fernandina Beach, which greatly contributed to our ease of transition. Andy's only backward glance of regret was leaving his beloved banana trees. After years of cultivation they were flourishing and abundant. We were assured that though bananas didn't grow in this more northern climate, oranges and lemons flourished.

Years later during a summer in New York State, when Andy was in the full throes of Alzheimer's, we sat on the porch companionably drinking a cup of coffee, enjoying the spectacular view over the valley. Andy's cat jumped up on his lap, purring loudly. Within minutes, both Andy and the cat were asleep. Testing, I called his name and heard no answer. This was my chance to hurriedly clean the bathroom. I hastily mopped, put away the pail and returned to the porch. GONE!

No sign of Andy or the cat. I checked up in the big garage, but there was no sight of him anywhere. The familiar cold chill of fear began engulfing me. More frightened and desperate by the minute, I got in the car and drove up the road where he often walked. Still no sight of him. Down two more connecting roads. Nothing – not even the cat. Could he have gone into the woods? Now I was really panicking. North and south, the woods extended for miles, east and west for over 30 miles. Parking quickly, I ran to the edge of the woods and called as loudly as I could. I called over and over. Finally I heard a faint answer from far away. So relieved, I called, "Andy. Come home!" Another faint answer, I stood at the edge of the woods and continued calling so he could find the direction by my voice. Over and over I shouted, "Andy, come home." I called and called for what seemed like hours and gradually his answers came closer. Finally, he emerged from the woods, his hands covered in blood, and more blood trickling from a cut on his forehead. His jeans were muddy and ripped at the knees.

He explained. "I fell down and couldn't get up. I've been hunting for the cat. She ran off and I can't find her. Come help me find her."

I was weak with relief. So many dangerous possibilities had been haunting me. Here he was, banged up, but not lost. My relief was tinged with sadness: he *was* still lost. Lost in his mind. "Come on in the house. We'll put Purssy's food out and she'll come home." Almost frantic, himself, he asked, "Are you sure?" "Yes, absolutely." Sure enough, later in the day Purssy was asleep on Andy's chair on the porch.

Later, while Andy took a much-needed nap, I relaxed on the porch with a comforting cup of tea. I heard two of the neighboring men laughing. Their loud voices carried as they amused each other with varying pitched cries of, "Andy, come home." Over and over their voices mocking my desperate cries. I leaned back in my rocker as I squeezed back tears. One man's pain is another man's amusement.

A few days later, after 2 hours at water aerobics, I came home lugging in groceries. "Come help me! I bought a ton and I need help carrying." No response. I did a quick check of the sunny porch where he usually sat. No Andy. I checked bedrooms and the bathroom—surely he was asleep in the back bedroom, where I'd sometimes found him. Suddenly, I heard the loud blast of a horn. A big four-wheel-drive pickup was in the driveway. There was another blast of the horn.

A uniformed game warden glared at me, "I found this man wandering over in the forest. Does he live here?"

Flooded with relief, I helped Andy down from the huge truck. "Yes, thank you for bringing him home."

Brusque and obviously disgusted with me, he showed me Andy's business card with our address and phone number. "If it hadn't been for this, I couldn't have brought him home. Don't let him go over there again, there are deep ponds he could slip into, not to mention water moccasins and rattlesnakes. Also, it's hunting season and some of those guys shoot at anything that moves. Shoot first and look later. JUST KEEP HIM HOME!"

As we went into the house, I sent up a silent prayer. "Help me, Lord. Help me. I really need Your help." I knew the Lord answers prayers of desperation, and I was desperate.

## GETTING SOME MUCH-NEEDED HELP

Charles, our friend from church stopped by often to sit with Andy on the porch, drink coffee and chat. On one such visit, Andy excused himself and went to take a nap. I shared my concerns with Charles and he suggested Hospice might be of help. I protested: to me, Hospice was a last resort when someone was near death. I pictured someone who holds your hand as your loved one takes their last gasps. Charles chuckled. "That's what most people think. Actually, Hospice is more about quality-of-life than death."

"Charles, the truth is, I just can't afford any more expenses right now," I told him. He sighed, "That's another misconception. Hospice is available to anyone, regardless of the ability to pay for services." I had my doubts. "Charles, Andy is still pretty active. I don't see the need for Hospice right now."

"Clearly you don't understand," he said. "Hospice could relieve a lot of your stress. For instance, a nurse or doctor is on call 24 hours a day. They're on call day or night." I had to admit, most of our crises occurred in the middle of the night or early morning, never conveniently during office hours.

"Are you telling me doctors or nurses are available any time of day or night?"

"Yes, not only doctors or nurses, but a Chaplain who will schedule visits if you want. This is strictly on a request basis, nothing to sign up for unless you want it. The nurse will also keep an eye on any medical equipment that needs monitoring. Andy is on oxygen isn't he?" Charles asked.

I was beginning to see some of my stress might be eliminated by Hospice. "I'll admit, sometimes I'm uncertain when the oxygen flow should be increased or decreased. You know, Charles, I'm reluctant to have Hospice because I just have the feeling like I'd be giving up on Andy and expecting him to keel over, a last resort, giving up."

Charles had such a gentle manner as he explained, "Actually, they can provide the tools and help to extend life more comfortably for Andy and for you. They can supply wheelchairs, hospital beds, even walkers or any variety of special equipment." As Charles explained I realized my impression of Hospice as the "end of the road, last-ditch effort" was far from the reality of their function. As Charles stood up and prepared to leave, he said, "They also have a short respite service for caregivers who need a break. It's a nursing home situation where the patient is placed a few days to a week to give the caregiver a break. Sometimes just a breathing spell to keep on keeping on."

With some reluctance I replied, "You've convinced me. What's the first step?"

"It's real simple. A doctor or nurse will come and evaluate Andy's needs and set up a schedule for a nurse to come by once a week – or less – and that's it."

In no time, Maizie, an efficient, cheerful nurse, was coming for a weekly visit. She took Andy's vitals. Sometimes she massaged his feet. Most importantly, she laughed at his jokes.

At my request, a chaplain, Chester, dropped by a few times a month. He was a very quiet, almost timid man who Andy took an instant liking to. Always dressed in a suit and tie, he was Andy's picture of the ideal preacher. On his first visit, I asked if he wanted me present or preferred a one-on-one. He preferred one-on-one. These visits usually happened on our shady porch. I could hear their quiet murmurs and occasional outbursts of laughter. Good medicine indeed.

Despite all my misgivings, Hospice proved to be the stress-reliever I needed. Just knowing I could call for help in the middle of the night was a great comfort. In reality, I never needed to call, but just knowing that I *could* provided comfort.

Charles assured me that there were many other aspects of Hospice; basically to be of help for caregivers trying to cope in the late stage of life. I wasn't ready to admit we were in a late stage, but I was grateful for the help.

Andy became a familiar sight traveling the back roads in his red pickup, searching for just the right stone for his fence.

CREDIT: Nathan Tavares

This white fawn seen near the New York home was a twin to a conventional brown twin. Specific to upstate New York, white deer are variants on common white-tailed deer, not albino.

CREDIT: Gary Johnson

A close-up of the now-grown-up white fawn, Snowflake.

CREDIT: Gary Johnson

Turkeys on parade with a hen, chicks and a "lookout" friend. A common sight in the New York yard.

CREDIT: Lorraine Pakkala

Bay of Fundy, where the sea rises so abruptly people are often caught in the swirling water.

CREDIT: ©GVictoria / Adobe Stock

My daughter, Cheryl, on holiday in Key West.

CREDIT: Shelly Mix

One of the captivating acts at the Sunset Pier in Key West is the cat trained to jump through a flaming hoop. You could almost see her smile as she sailed through the air!

CREDIT: Shelly Mix

House Boat Row in Key West on a calm day.
CREDIT: State Archives of Florida/McDonald

This bewhiskered gentleman with the polydactyl feet is a permanent resident of the Hemingway House.
CREDIT: © spiritofamerica / Adobe Stock

Lorraine's beloved friends at the Alzheimer's Caregivers Support Group at Nassau County Council on the Aging.

CREDIT: Melanie J. Ferreira

# Chapter Six

## Hurdles

Red letter day! My daughter Cheryl took Andy on a trip to his alma mater, Ithaca College, where he'd graduated as salutatorian in 1953. They slowly traversed Alumni Hall. The staff honored his status as an alum and treated him like gold. They ate in the dining hall, where Andy was in his element. He was gallant, dressed in his four-button cuff sports coat, paying for lunch with a flourish of his platinum credit card, and leaving a big tip. All things he loved to do.

Both Cheryl and Andy had a lovely day. He didn't monitor her driving, shout at red lights, or scream about oncoming traffic as he did with me. At the end of the day, he seemed his dear, old self, and declared it "A perfect day!" He added, "Things aren't like they used to be. When I was a student, classrooms were strung all over Ithaca. Sometimes we had to walk blocks from one class to another. It was not the beautiful campus we toured today. No, things aren't like they used to be."

So many things weren't like they used to be. Andy was falling down frequently and experiencing increasing incontinence. I guess I'd just attributed it to the natural aging process, but in fact these are signs of the Alzheimer's decline. He began sleeping a lot in the daytime, even though I tried to discourage it because then he wouldn't sleep at night.

When Andy had been in Depends for about two years, I sat at the kitchen table clipping coupons for them. Andy sat across from me drinking coffee and soaking his biscotti. Clipping away, I remarked, "This is a really good deal, a dollar off." Slurping fast before his biscotti disintegrated, then catching his breath, he remarked, "I suppose I'll come to that someday. But for now I really like the padded underwear you get me."

## SO MUCH FOR ADULT DAY CARE

Several in the caregivers group brought their loved ones to "Adult Day Care" for several hours on weekdays. I filled out the forms and went in with Andy a few days later. I left as he was animatedly in conversation with a well-dressed gentleman about his age. Andy seemed at ease in his four-button cuff sports coat, white shirt and tie – the two men seemed equally professional. I left for water aerobics, content he was enjoying himself with a rare opportunity to chat with a peer. When I returned a few hours later, I unashamedly peeked in the window before going in. He was still deep in conversation, animated and smiling. I was so optimistic and filled with hope as we left. He was smiling and shaking hands all around. In the car, red-faced with rage, doing a complete about-face, he screamed at me, "Don't ever take me to that hellhole again."

Surprised, I answered, "What? I thought you enjoyed talking to that nice man."

He was so enraged he could barely talk. "He was old! All of them were old! OLD PEOPLE! I can't stand old people. Don't ever take me there again! Just let me stay home with my dog and cat and enjoy life. No more old people."

"Andy," I said, "we don't have a cat or dog." He was still red-faced with rage. "Just let me stay home. No more old people and that's it!" So much for adult day care.

## DRIVING

A recurring problem for many caregivers is the issue of driving. When the question comes up about their ability to drive, few Alzheimer's patients will admit to any problem. One caregiver was awakened by his bedside phone ringing at 3 a.m. Picking up, he noticed his wife's bed was empty. The reason soon became apparent. She was on her cell phone and pleaded, "Come find me, I can't find my way home." Instantly fully awake and fully alert, he realized she'd taken the car keys from his pants pocket. She was probably miles away by now. He asked, "Are there any street signs you can see?" Between sobs she answered, "No, it's all dark. I'm on a dirt road and there are lots of woods."

Trying to comfort her, he said, "Drive very slowly until you see some sign, then stop and tell me what it says." He listened and heard the crunch of gravel for what seemed an eternity. Finally she exclaimed, "It says Bull Hill." He realized she was about ten miles from home. "Now stop the car. Don't drive any more. Just stay there and I'll come and get you." He jumped into his pickup and went to her rescue. He learned the lesson: hide the car keys. She loved to get in the car and drive. She claimed it was her only freedom, the only place she was in control.

Thankfully, I didn't have that problem with Andy. In New York he enjoyed driving the trails through the woods in his rugged all-terrain vehicle (ATV). The four-wheeler was great for narrow trails and steep inclines, and he spent hours exploring the creeks and trails near our home. In the early days of Alzheimer's, he got on his ATV for a trail ride. Suddenly, I heard a crash. I rushed out to find him on the ground beside his overturned vehicle. Fortunately, two neighbors also heard the crash and were beside him before I reached him. Helping him up, my neighbor said, "He's just shook up, no broken bones."

Later at the house, Andy reached in his pocket and handed me his keys. "I'm never driving again. If I'd been in a car on the road, I could have killed somebody. My reflexes are way off. I thought I was driving between two trees and I smashed right into one. If those had been cars, I would have killed somebody." Just that positively, Andy gave up driving. It never came up again and he never expressed any desire to drive after that.

I often heard horror stories of loved ones insisting on driving when their ability was non-existent. One husband forced the keys from his wife and, before she could stop him, he roared off in a blaze of dust. She called the state police and gave the license number, only hoping he would be stopped before a tragedy occurred. Not long after, troopers stopped him on I-95 going the wrong way on the highway. Her only recourse was to not only hide the car keys, but to padlock the garage. Yes, thankfully I didn't have that hurdle.

I did have other hurdles. Andy still loved to eat out, and a nearby rib shack was one of his favorites. After giving our order one day, Andy announced he needed to use the bathroom. It was difficult for him to locate the men's room in a strange place, so I accompanied him. I sat at a nearby table and people-watched. I noticed a well-dressed man in suit and tie leave his car and head for the restroom. He came out quickly, returned to his car, and drove off without ordering. Several minutes later Andy came out and we returned to our table. When the waiter delivered our sauce-dripping meal, Andy stared at him intently, "Oh no," Andy said, "I made a horrible mistake." Used to his outbreaks by now, I calmly asked, "What's the problem?" Andy picked up his fork and started eating, "Our waiter is wearing a T-shirt and jeans. I thought he had on a suit and tie. I just gave a man in suit and tie a fifty-dollar bill in the bathroom to pay for our meal. I gave it to a man in a suit and tie." That explained the rush of the man who left without ordering a meal. Andy was very distraught. "I just can't be trusted with money anymore. I can't believe I did that."

As he grew more disturbed by the minute, I tried to soothe him. "It's a mistake anybody could make. Let's just forget it and eat." By the end of our meal, he had forgotten it.

Back home, he was ready for his afternoon nap. His wallet was on the bedside table where he always placed it. When I was sure he was asleep, I quietly took it. I replaced the three fifty dollar bills with ten one dollar bills and put it back on the table. He never noticed or commented. A brilliant accountant, not noticing when a hundred and fifty dollars disappeared from his wallet.

A few days later, Andy sat mumbling in his chair by the window, very intent and absorbed in a nearly inaudible conversation. I asked, "What are you saying? I can barely hear you." I received a dismissive hand gesture. "Leave me alone, I'm talking to myself. Just leave me alone."

Later, going to bed, he asked, "What year did Emil die? My own brother, and I can't even remember when he died."

I pondered a few minutes, "Well, let me see, it was 1994 so I guess it was about 18 years ago. Acting surprised, he said, "I talked to him all day today. Each time I asked him when he died, he wouldn't answer me. Other than that we had a good talk."

I asked, "Did you see Emil?" He instantly replied, "Yes, of course I saw him. We talked all day." The by now familiar claw of cold fright clutched my heart.

The caregivers group became the only place I shared these abnormalities. I didn't want to frighten my children, and in the back of my mind was the possibility that my caregiving was inadequate and he'd be removed to a strange environment and live in deep fear. I retained an overwhelming respect for the person he really was beneath the tangle of Alzheimer's. Somewhere, my dear, brilliant Andy did still dwell. At the group, I was assured other loved ones, too, spent hours mumbling but did not often share their conversations with family. The director told me mumbling for hours was a common Alzheimer's trait.

I'd become concerned when Andy, who'd previously spent hours piecing together complex jigsaw puzzles, had lately grown frustrated and threw them violently to the floor and gave up in a rage. I learned from the group that huge 1000-piece puzzles were too much to grasp, while 500- to-300 were still doable. Sure enough, the smaller ones were still enjoyable to Andy. It became a good way for him to interact when my daughters, Cheryl and Shelly, came to visit. They spent hours laughing and joking, triumphant when an errant piece found a home. Andy was amiable and had fun retelling his old jokes as they pieced together the puzzles.

Andy was disoriented most of the time. We celebrated one quiet New Year's Eve at home. He seemed relaxed and mellow until he started pacing and said, "I'm looking for my guitar. I laid it down and now I can't find it. And I can't find the key to this motel room. Do you have the key? Do you know where I laid my guitar?" This was followed by hours of asking me over and over if I had the room key and did I know where his guitar was. He has never owned or played a guitar. Finally, he was distracted when our neighborhood exploded in fireworks and shotguns going off as the New Year was ushered in with a bang.

On New Year's Day, 2012, Andy insisted it was 2004. He looked at me during our early morning coffee and asked, "Milli, when did we drive down here from Rochester? How did we get here?" I patiently explained, "I'm not Milli, and drink your coffee." Sometimes I was forced to pretend I was Milli, but not today. I was reluctant to be someone else on this first day of a new year.

Even more disturbing lately were Andy's reports of "evil little people" who he said would fill the room and mock and jeer him. He claimed they called him stupid, an old fool, and screamed at him. Sometimes he came out of the bathroom and accused me of making fun of him. Of course, I didn't. He often spoke of those people and told me there are many and they fill up the house. One night he asked where we would sleep. I answered, "In our beds." He appeared frantic. "We can't – they're all full of these people. I think they're your friends from church. I don't know any of them and you are chit-chatting with them and encouraging them to stay. I'm asking you, where will we sleep?" I tried to soothe him. As frightening as it was for me, I could appreciate how terrorizing it must be for him.

One afternoon, I found him all crunched up on a small couch in the back bedroom trying to nap. He explained, "I'm here because all the other beds are full of people I don't know." Looking around, he asked, "Where did all the Jewish people go? This house was wall-to-wall Jews. Where did they go?"

"Who knows?" I replied. "Anyway, now it's just us. Let's have coffee on the porch and watch the hummingbirds." We relaxed with our hot coffee and he asked, "I've got a question. Where did you learn to cook Jewish Kosher? They all keep raving about your great food and how they admire that you keep a Kosher Kitchen. Where did you learn it?" I just shrugged. "Oh, I don't remember. I must have picked it up somewhere." He continued to talk about the "Jewish people" most of the day.

At that time, he recalled a pleasant experience he and Milli had. At least I'm assuming it was an experience they had. He said, "Milli, remember that funny time at the Houston airport when you just grabbed up our luggage and got on the plane when they said we couldn't? You were spectacular. You said come on and we just piled in." He chuckled at the remembrance.

In my persona of Milli, I answered, "Oh, yeah, Andy. That was fun." I no longer wrestle with the wifely jealousy that once consumed me. Now my attitude is, *Who cares as long as he isn't belligerent for a few hours?* Of course I strictly adhere to Dr. P's advice to "never argue with an Alzheimer's patient."

Through all the hurdles, the once-a-month Alzheimer's group was a very good way for me to keep a grasp on reality. Compared to the other loved ones, I realized how fortunate I was that Andy showered himself and changed his clothes with no argument or problem. This was not usually the case with several other wives or husbands. Some dealt with everyday resistance even to get their loved ones to shower, requiring help from paid home-health aides. Some caregivers reported their loved ones insists on wearing the same clothes day after day and oppose a change of clothes even when the current ones became crusty.

I especially admired the several men who were patiently caring for wives or mothers. They monitored their cooking attempts and faced all the daily obstacles I was facing. One son had an escape-proof fence built around his house before moving his father from out-of-state to share his home. A former administrator, he took over the reins of the household, even dictating his son's bedtime. "Nine o'clock to bed and no back talk." After his father was asleep, he'd creep into the living room and turn the TV to its lowest volume. It didn't always work, and many times he was forced to go to bed in the middle of a program. He'd learned the hard lesson we'd all succumbed to, you never win an argument with Alzheimer's patients.

Another common complaint among us caregivers was the daily battle over meals and administering pills. During one tantrum, Andy yelled at me, "Wait till you get old! Having somebody nagging and fussing over you constantly is no fun. Wait till you get old!" I was wise enough to keep my mouth shut. I can only hope to get the loving care he received from me, someone to keep track of seven prescriptions, the reordering, the organizing, and the forcing – yes, forcing – him to take them. He had only to walk to the table where I tried to prepare his favorite foods, then forced and cajoled him to eat. Yes, I could only hope my old age would be as pleasant as his. Old age? Only four-years-older than me, he thought I was a kid.

One day I read in my Bible, "Problems too big for me are piled higher than my head. My only hope is in your love and faithfulness." *(Psalm 40:12)*. That was for sure, problems too big for me to solve. I would just have to take them one day at a time. I couldn't think of tomorrow or I'd be overwhelmed. Sunk.

My only hope at times was God's love and faithfulness - an only hope, yes, but promised with love and faithfulness.

# Chapter Seven

# Caregivers

Our friend Charles held out what proved to be an absolute lifesaver for me. "There's a lady at church, Evelyn, who just retired and is looking for a part-time job. Maybe she'd be a good fit for you. Help you out a few days a week." And what a help she was! I was truly rescued. Often in times of desperation, I'd prayed, "Help me Lord, help me." The caregiving helpers the Lord sent were the answer to that plea.

Evelyn arrived sipping a big cup of cappuccino and wearing a huge smile. Pert and petite, her face was framed by an elfin haircut and laughing eyes. Cheerful and competent, she joined us on the back porch. I knew better than to announce to Andy that someone was coming to "babysit" him. I introduced her only as a friend of mine. She was soon settled in the big chair, laughing largely at Andy's jokes. He appeared animated and jolly, delighted to have a new audience for his timeworn jokes. In the midst of the laughter, I touched Andy lightly on the shoulder and said I had to run an errand. He barely noticed I was leaving.

The arrangement with Evelyn was five hours twice a week at $10 an hour. This was ample time for me to get my much-needed water aerobic exercise so essential in keeping my knees moving; do banking; go grocery shopping; in short, keep the household functioning and my sanity intact. Evelyn seemed to know instinctively just how to handle Andy. She never treated him as a child, never talked down to him, and always treated him with respect. When he grew restless, she suggested a walk around the neighborhood, roughly a mile. He often took a nap after that. He never cursed her or argued with her over meals or eating, a blessing I didn't enjoy.

Most importantly, I could leave Andy without the tension and worry that was well-founded. Once, before Evelyn came, on my return, I'd found Andy with a metal screwdriver attacking the electric water heater in the garage. "There's something wrong with this damn heater, I couldn't get any hot water for my shower."

I knew the lack of hot water was because he'd forgotten to turn the faucet far enough. "Let's go in and test it again." After this, I made a point of turning the water on for him. He resisted and protested, but I did it anyway.

Another time, he used a hatchet to hack the soil around our septic pump, thinking he was fixing the plumbing. The plumber was totally perplexed. "I don't understand how this could happen, but somehow the electric connection underground is severed," he told me. I didn't enlighten him as I paid the $500 fee to get it fixed.

Hopefully, with Evelyn there, it meant no more risky ventures – or so I hoped.

One day, Andy noticed the dishwasher was full of dirty dishes. He asked Evelyn's assistance in turning on the water after he'd poured in a half bottle of liquid detergent. Satisfied it was swishing away, they retired to the living room to watch Polka Time on RFD TV. During a commercial, Evelyn peeked into the kitchen and, to her horror, found the room knee deep in suds. "Andy, we did something wrong. Look!"

He rushed into the bathroom and gathered up all the clean towels and together they sopped up the mess. When I came home a few hours later they were both calmly porch-sitting. I noticed how gleaming clean the kitchen floor was and when they explained, we all shared a hearty laugh. Andy was so personable and social, Evelyn had no reason to mistrust his judgment. At this time, he appeared perfectly normal in any social situation. Several doubted he had any problem and a few claimed Lorraine was the one mixed up. The cursing, screaming, and tantrums were reserved for me alone.

## AN INDESCENT PROPOSAL

One day, Andy sat on the edge of the tub watching me put on my makeup. I could sense he had something on his mind. After much hemming and hawing, he asked, "How would you feel if I propositioned Evelyn?" Carefully stroking mascara on my lashes, I replied, "I'd be furious, and so would she. Don't even attempt it." Not at all deterred, he continued, "I know she'd love to have sex with me. She's single and just dying for sex."

I responded, "Andy, get it out of your head that all single women are dying for sex. She's not only *not* dying for sex, she'd probably be so mad she'd never come back. Don't ask her!" Andy got very stubborn and with a set to his mouth said, "I can at least ask."

"Andy, I know this is a precept difficult for you to accept, but some women are single precisely because they don't want sex." I met Evelyn at the door and warned her when she arrived. She was nonchalant, not shocked, "I know how to handle it. He loves to walk, we'll just take a long walk and he'll forget it."

Later that day, my dental floss spiraled to an end. I rummaged in Andy's sink drawer for one of his endless supply of floss. This came under the heading of his "whatever is worth doing is worth doing to excess." There was a bottle of blue triangle-shaped pills, half empty. Oh no! Viagra. How many had he taken? His theory of, "if one is good, three is better," could kill him. I dumped them in the toilet and flushed, carrying the empty bottle out to the garbage can in the garage. Thankful for the twenty-minute attention span, I hoped he'd never miss them. For the next few days, he was very unsteady on his feet and clutched at furniture to keep his balance as he walked. I attributed it to Viagra, but who knew?

Evelyn was always cheerful and patient, seemed to know how to handle Andy. Sometimes when I couldn't talk him out of a notion to search the cemetery or undertake a long walk in the rain, she could. She was clearly an answer to my plea—"Help me, Lord, help me."

It's absolutely essential to have someone who can relieve you as a caregiver for at least one day a week, two days would be even better. I was overwhelmingly exhausted all of the time. Besides the need to be always on the alert and watchful, there is the emotional toll as you see your loved one slip deeper and deeper into paranoia and lose cognizance. The heartrending reality of daily slippage is exhausting. The time I spent in the pool was a great stress reliever. Each caregiver can find their own best stress reliever. Sometimes just strolling through a shopping center can be a refresher – well-known as retail therapy.

I was so fortunate when my son, Walt, moved near us in Florida. A mere four miles away, he often popped in and took Andy on long walks. Andy loved to walk. One of their favorite walks was a nature trail in the middle of the city of Fernandina Beach, a wild nature preserve that skirts Egan's Creek Greenway with large Spanish moss-draped live oaks. It offers great wildlife viewing, home to the gopher turtle, deer, raccoons, and alligators. Their prized sighting was to see an alligator lying in the sun. They were seldom disappointed.

Another favorite walk was along the ocean with miles of white sandy beach. Here they sometimes saw dolphins bobbing near the shore. Andy returned from these walks animated and refreshed. Usually two hours later he'd complain we never went to the ocean anymore. Walter was patient and very respectful of Andy, even though his occasional flights of fantasy may have been far out.

When we returned to New York State for the summer, Cheryl's friend Maria agreed to be Andy's companion one day a week. This meant I had to find someone else for one other day each week, as I required two days in the pool per week for my knees' sake.

Coming home when Maria was with Andy, I often found them speaking rapidly and avidly in Finnish. She'd originally come from Finland about ten years before and Finnish was her native language. As a child, Andy didn't learn to speak English until he attended school. He declared he had forgotten how to converse in Finnish, but soon he and Maria conversed fluently. All of Andy's childhood language came back to him. I could see he didn't hesitate or have to ponder as he and Maria enjoyed their back and forth banter in Finnish.

Of all people, Maria most admired the 70-foot long stone fence Andy built. He was four years building it and it was truly a work of art. He had traveled the back roads in his little red Toyota pickup and scrounged creek beds, old fences, and ditches for just the perfect rock. During the building of the 4-foot wide stone fence, his cat Purssy accompanied him daily and sat on the fence as though encouraging him. As faithful as a paid employee, she sat day after day, watching closely as he worked, following at his heels wherever he went. These were the lovely golden days before Alzheimer's. I didn't even know the word "Alzheimer's."

On one of these sunny days when the whole earth seemed flooded in a golden light, Andy had a suggestion. He urged me to accompany him as he planned to go to a choice spot. It was an abandoned farm complete with a sturdy barn, crumbling house, and fruit trees gone wild. Ruts from long-ago wagon trails were still visible, and remnants of an old smoke house and an outdoor privy still stood. Hop vines draped the walnut trees surrounding the homestead. If you stood still, you could almost hear the voices of long ago.

We rambled through the still-sturdy old barn. Every hand-hewn beam and creaking floorboard seemed to tell a story. Three old grain bins were polished smooth as glass from years of storing buckwheat, corn, and wheat, fodder stored against the harsh New York winters for the chickens, cows, and horses that used to shelter there. Behind the horse stalls, cracked leather harnesses still hung from pegs. If you shut your eyes, you could almost hear the whinnying and stamping hooves of those long ago horses.

As we sat on the low stone fence amid the swirling leaves and golden light, Andy said, "Just think, a hundred years ago this was a productive farm, almost a village in itself. I can tell this was a prosperous farm." Mindful of the beauty and peace surrounding us, I asked, "How can you possibly tell this was a prosperous farm?" He leaned over and gave me a quick hug. "Because I'm psychic," he joked. I wasn't satisfied with this answer. "No really, what makes you think this was a prosperous farm?"

"Just look around you. The hops were used in brewing beer so they had some time for leisure sipping. There are intricate stone ditches to bring water not only to the house and barn, but to the garden, too. The details of ditches and stone fences indicate the work of more than one man, so they must have had hired help. Four stalls in the barn means they had two teams of horses, possibly a team of sturdy work horses and maybe a team of sleek, fast-moving horses to pull a buggy. All those cow stalls indicate they may have sold butter and milk products. And the large size of the smokehouse also speaks of plenty." The remnants of a fallen-down doghouse stood between the house and barn. Andy glanced at it. "Probably a good farm dog kept the coyotes and bears away."

I shuddered at the mention of bears and coyotes. I'd almost forgotten they still roamed in this remote forest. I looked over at Andy sitting beside me, still handsome at 69, with thinning gray hair and a stunning physique. He was slim and muscular due to his habit of walking two to five miles a day. Not a deliberate regime, but because he really loved to walk and observe nature. He was the picture of health. Neither of us could have dreamed of what lay ahead.

Maria, my New York helper, was constructing a rock garden at her home and recognized a stone genius when she saw one. On the days she spent with Andy, they could hardly wait for me to leave and would be in her car driving on a hunt for the perfect stone for her garden. When I came home she'd show me the back seat of her car piled high with stones, so high I feared for her axles. Andy remembered every stone pile, rock outcropping, and ditch where stones were ripe for the picking. They had such fun traveling the back roads searching for their trophies.

At times, when I arrived home they'd be in the living room with the TV turned to an exuberant evangelist. They'd be singing and clapping to the music. In genuine enthusiasm and joy, they were singing and worshipping. The scriptures tell us to worship in spirit and truth, and they were truly worshipping. The Bible teaches, "So shall my word be that goeth out of my mouth: it shall not return unto me void, but it shall accomplish that which I please…" *(Isaiah 55:11, KJV)*. They were experiencing "The Living Word."

Andy was very present during these times, but twenty minutes after Maria left he didn't know she'd been there. Since she could only come one day a week, I turned to Ike, a friend from church, who was recuperating from a painful back problem. A forty-something with a wife and three children and a former rugged outdoorsman, I doubted he'd be interested in being a companion to Andy. When I approached him about attending Andy one day a week, we agreed we'd try it. It proved to be a very good fit for both Andy and Ike.

A male companion was a wonderful change for Andy. He loved expounding to Ike about investment opportunities. They were both avid in their interest in sports. This was an opportunity for Andy to discuss football with a knowledgeable fellow enthusiast. Soon, Ike's pickup arriving in the driveway was a welcome sight. They developed a deep mutual respect for each other. Despite Andy's ever growing Alzheimer's, he was more his old self when Ike was there.

It's very important *not* to use the word "babysitter" to your loved one. It's demeaning and reduces the patient to an unhealthy level. It's probably wiser not to mention directly that you are leaving them in someone else's care. The sense of independence and respect should be maintained in this tricky shared caregiving. However, keep firmly in mind that you do need respite time for yourself.

# Chapter Eight

# Sex

There was a stage when, each time I returned from water aerobics or a quick grocery trip, Andy accused me of having a boyfriend, being with a boyfriend, or plotting with a boyfriend. "I know you're starved for sex and I'm not blaming you. I just want you to admit it," he said.

*No, I'm not starved for sex. I'm starved for conversation, a real conversation. My every attempt at conversation ends in a worn-out joke, or a blank stare followed by, "I don't know what you're talking about." If I ever fantasize, it's about* conversation, *not sex.*

Even touching Andy's *feet* became a task I struggled with. When I attempted to cut his toenails, he would jerk away, kicking and saying I was hurting him. In general not a pretty picture. Finally, I gave up. There was a pedicure shop next to our grocery store that advertised $20 pedicures as opposed to a $50 co-pay with our insurance for a foot doctor.

We set out in the car, heading to the shop with much instruction as to when to stop, when to go, and "I think you're going in the wrong direction." Once inside, young ladies in sweeping, ornate gold dresses hovered as they removed Andy's shoes and placed his feet in the whirling footbath. He settled back, closed his eyes and appeared to be half asleep. This was far more peaceful than our previous physical struggles. "How long does this take?" I asked. When I heard about 45 minutes, I figured this was a good time to run next door and do some quick grocery shopping. When I returned, the three tiny girls were smiling and bowing, some busy clipping other customers' nails. Andy was in an expansive mood, feet dried and clipped. He opened his wallet with a flourish and left a $10 tip. So much for saving money.

Chewing our sandwiches on the back porch, Andy leaned toward me. "Thanks, that was wonderful. Just what I needed." I took a long swig of coffee before I answered. "Yes. Your toenails were really long." He shook his head no, "I mean the lovely, sexy things those Geisha girls did to me."

"Andy, they just cut your toenails. Nothing more."

He was exasperated with me, "No, no, I mean the wonderful, sexy things those girls did to me. Geisha girls are very talented and know just how to please a man." Now I was exasperated, "They just cut your toenails, Andy. After all, there were at least three other customers there. Nothing sexual happened. You got your toenails cut. Period!" He got a sly look, "I know better, those girls are trained from birth on how to please a man. It's their main purpose in life. I know from personal experience they really do know how to please a man."

I belatedly remembered to never argue with an Alzheimer's patient, they are never wrong. You can never win. They never hold a grudge, however, I did want to get in the last word. "Andy, they just cut your toenails." He assumed his sly, know-it-all smile. "Toenails grow. There'll be a next time." He had the last word after all.

I truly relished my first cup of coffee the next morning. "I wonder what could replace that wonderful first sip of coffee when we get to heaven?" Andy gave me a sly glance, "I can live without coffee. But what could God have that would possibly replace sex?" I cradled my mug and answered, "Well, He invented sex and coffee, I'm sure something more wonderful awaits us." Andy took a long sip, "I'm not so sure."

My enjoyment for sex diminished at the same rate that Andy's knowledge of who I was diminished. As Andy knew who I was less and less, the day came when I gave it up. Not without protest from Andy, but his twenty-minute attention span in this one instance was helpful. The physical sharing of our love had been a rich, enjoyable aspect of our marriage, but like so many things Alzheimer's robbed us of, this too was no longer true.

I tried to remember that Andy was a thoughtful, loving, and considerate husband before Alzheimer's reduced him to a petulant child racked often with four-year-old tantrums. I kept in the forefront the wonderful, witty, dearly-loved companion he'd been for more than seventeen years. I tried to treat him with the respect due the wonderful person he really was/is.

## THE MEETING

I hate meetings; avoid them like the plague. The greatest blessing of my retirement is I no longer need to attend long, boring meetings. So when my friend Merilee approached me to join her committee, I instantly declined with the excuse of needing to be with Andy in the evenings. "We meet at noon, a brief hour," Merilee told me, "and believe me, it's anything but boring." I ran out of excuses and agreed to once a week, noon to one, and only for six weeks. I probably needed to step out of the caregiving role briefly, if nothing else.

As promised, the meetings were stimulating and brief. In the coffee hour following, I often engaged in lively conversation with others and enjoyed especially sparring with Melvin. He was a sharp dresser with brown eyes that often became almost black when the subject turned intense. I noticed a stray lock from his thick black hair that often covered his left eye if he didn't brush it aside. The six weeks of the committee finally came to a close. As usual, Mel and I got into a deep conversation. When I looked up, I realized everyone else had left. Only Mel and I lingered over coffee. I gathered up notebook and purse, ready to leave.

Mel started to shuffle papers into his briefcase, then turned to me. "Let's meet once a week for conversation, I so enjoy talking to you. Could we meet just for coffee? No pressure, just conversation. Maybe just for an hour, like the meetings." He looked at me expectantly and brushed away that stray lock of hair.

Standing there with the prospect of a real conversation with someone with the quickness and agility of a brilliant person seemed very tempting. I also knew instinctively it wasn't "just coffee." Reluctantly, I declined, "I really haven't time. Andy requires my full-time commitment."

He turned and looked at me fully, "Do you understand I find you overwhelmingly attractive, overwhelmingly irresistible? I want to see you again. Hey, it's just coffee. If you cared for me, you could give me just an hour. I value your qualities of understanding, intelligence, and maturity. If you cared more, you'd give me an hour."

*Land of Forgetfulness*

To say I was intrigued was an understatement, but tempted to pursue it further, not so much. I looked at him, really looked at him, memorizing the stray lock of hair that kept falling over his left eye, the slight cleft of the chin, and the deep well of those dark brown eyes. "You're wrong, if I cared *less,* I could give you an hour."

I turned to leave when unexpectedly he bent way down and gathered me in his arms. I was swept up into an embrace. As his arms tightened around me I smelled the tantalizing piney scent of his aftershave, almost intoxicating, then a long kiss on my lips. I amazed myself with my reaction. I didn't pull away. Finally, he held me at arm's length, "I've been wanting to do that for such a long time."

"Really?" I was taken totally by surprise. Another surprise, I wasn't as dead to sex as I'd thought.

Then he turned abruptly, grabbed his briefcase and hurriedly left. I listened as the sound as his footsteps grew fainter and fainter and finally the loud slamming door. I ran to my car through a heavy downpour. The lights went on as I started the car. It was nearly dark at mid-day. I was accompanied by the lonely swish, swish of the wipers. Thinking over the past hour, I was suddenly hit with a wallop! Mel was Andy. Right down to the four-button sports coat cuff. That's why conversing with him was so stimulating. He had the sharp wit, extreme intelligence, and wry humor so endearing in Andy. Subtract ten or fifteen years and Mel was Andy. Being brutally honest with myself, I admitted, yes, I was totally taken by surprise.

I'd often heard the lament, "I just couldn't help myself. The temptation was overwhelming. I couldn't help myself. There was nothing I could do but give in." I found the simple truth of God's word proved true, "There hath no temptation taken you but such as is common to man; but God is faithful, who will not suffer you to be tempted above what you are able; but will with the temptation also make a way to escape, that you may be able to bear it." *(1 Corinthians 10:13, KJV).*

The minute I walked in the door at home, I was confronted with reality, or what passed for reality these days. Evelyn was waiting for me and left at the swinging of the door as I entered. "He's just impossible. I've had it, nothing pleases him today." With that, she left. Then I realized, Evelyn had always been attendant in broad daylight and bright sunshine. She had never witnessed "Sundowning" – a symptom where some people with

Alzheimer's have increased anxiety in the evening as the sun goes down. Andy always grew increasingly restless and more erratic at sundown, often obsessing over imagined insults, refusing to eat or take his medication, or paranoid that someone was after us. I was at a loss in coping with this. Sometimes his favorite country TV station would play old-time music or show tractor exhibits. These things sometimes helped, but not always. I also had to monitor programs carefully, as sometimes seemingly innocent shows such as *Columbo* could set off hours of distress, bad guys out to kill him, or people out in the bushes watching us, about to charge and attack us. "Where are my guns? Damn you, have you given away my guns? I can't find my guns. We have no protection," he'd scream.

When I realized Andy's "diminishment," I had his sons remove all guns from the house with the exception of a pump-air-gun that he used to scare away the squirrels. I'd heard horror stories of caregivers being shot in the dark when the loved one mistook them for a burglar. As time passed, I could see this as a real possibility as I often woke up in the middle of the night and found him wandering in search of an intruder. In the dark, a loved one looks exactly like an intruder.

Chances are, each family will find a way to cope with Sundowning, but I never found a consistent, effective coping mechanism. My immediate solution was to suggest we have a cup of coffee. He gave a dismissive hand gesture. "They're here already; they arrived while you were out. They've just stepped out to do some shopping. They'll be back any minute. Bob and Connie will be here any minute. Our best friends visiting, aren't you even excited?"

"Andy, nobody is here, you must have dreamed it," I said. Increasingly excited, he screamed, "But they're here already, our best friends, and they've driven all this way. We've got to fix them a great meal." Thinking I was Milli, he couldn't understand why I wasn't excited with him.

A half hour later, I'd convinced him I shouldn't cook up a feast for visitors. I didn't bother to un-sort that I wasn't Milli or that Bob had died a few years ago. As Andy finally settled down to work a puzzle, I fixed myself a hot cup of tea, debating if I should indulge in a biscotti. A great wave of loneliness washed over me. I analyzed my situation as my tea grew cold. *I've lost more than a sexual partner, I've lost a whole person. I'm in a spot where the closest person to me no longer cares what I say or do, with the added sadness that there is a warm, breathing, living body in the room that really isn't here.* I felt so alone in that room. I recalled a description I'd once read of Alzheimer's, "His mind appeared to be a kaleidoscope that had been so shaken that it couldn't regain its original pattern."

I let my mind wander to Mel's offer of "conversation once a week." As temptations go, what could be more tantalizing than the prospect of weekly conversation with a handsome, brilliant man who'd declared me "overwhelmingly desirable?" It was an intoxicating prospect, as strong as alcohol and just as addictive. I knew I had to absolutely turn away in obedience to Christ and in respect to my marriage vows to Andy. The Lord promised to make a way of escape. Was it a temptation to meet Mel once a week? Yes! But I was well aware of the attraction between us, the attraction that would grow if I nourished it. I knew that to be true to Andy and the Lord I must turn my back on this temptation. Besides my marriage vows, I also belong to the Lord, "Know ye not that ye are the temple of God, and that the Spirit of God dwelleth in you? *(1 Corinthians 3:16, KJV).*

The dictionary calls conversation "social intercourse." Andy accused me of desiring *sexual* intercourse, not a real temptation to me, but *social* intercourse, yes! It is a real temptation. However, the Holy Spirit helps us overcome anything and everything. It is also my experience that emotions don't diminish with age, but rather intensify.

# Chapter Nine

# Shopping Trip

More and more, Andy called me Milli, the name of his late wife. Sometimes when I said, "No, I'm Lorraine," he corrected me. "Lorraine was a jolly, cheerful person. You are nothing like Lorraine."

Gradually I noticed a pattern evolving – to my persona, Milli, Andy would bring up old grievances and arguments, often launching into these conflicts full blown. "Look, Milli, you are totally out of control. You've run up the credit card to $5,000. I got the bill yesterday. THIS HAS GOT TO STOP! Do you hear me? This has to stop."

Finally one day, I grasped his shoulders. "Andy, look me in the eyes, you are right. You are absolutely right. I promise, no more credit card bills." Once I had agreed with him aggressively, he seemed content to dismiss the subject – for a season. At various times he launched into tirades that apparently had been conflicts in marriage number one. Throughout the previous years of our by-now-eighteen-years-of-marriage, he had never once criticized his late wife. I'd assumed their marriage and lifestyle to be congenial and trouble-free. Over the next few months, Andy went verbally and in great detail over what I supposed to be every conflict he'd ever had with Milli, from the colleges their sons chose, to the detail of what he perceived as excess spending on their grandchildren. He spared no detail from the outrageous price of tiny dresses to complaints of Milli's smoking habit.

I learned the only way to curb the overpowering rages was to make him look me in the eyes and declare he was right – absolutely RIGHT. There'd be calm for a few days, then another conflict would surface. I mourned anew that these old conflicts alone were his memories.

In the meantime our day-to-day life continued. I attempted to adhere to life as we knew it, but life as we knew it was no more. A glaring example was our weekly shopping trip.

During one drive to the mall, Andy asked, "Are we taking the truck in for inspection? How come you don't let me drive the truck anymore? Oh shit! We're in the car, not the truck."

He rambled on with several outbursts of caution when a car approached and sporadically made urgent screams of "Stop!" and "Go!" at lights. Finally, we arrived at the mall parking lot. "Oh no! I'm wearing my bedroom slippers. Go back home, I've got to get my shoes." I tried a calming voice, "You'll be just fine, your slippers look just like Birkenstocks. Let's do a few minutes of shopping before we head home."

We went in with him mumbling and cursing, shuffling in his bedroom slippers. In a loud voice, he asked, "Why are we here? Where's the bathroom? I need a bathroom. Now!" Still trying for calm, I answered, "It's at the other end of the store. Look, here's the RID-X you wanted." He put three boxes in the cart. *Well, at least his theory "if one is good, three is better" hasn't changed*, I thought. I tried to put one back on the shelf. At $6 a box, I'd be short of cash for bread and milk.

He firmly restored the third box back into the cart. "Let me make *some* decisions. You boss my every move. Leave me alone! Where's the bathroom?" I had to escort him to the door, knowing he'd get lost and wander the whole store looking for me, or worse wander the parking lot searching for the car while I frantically searched for him. It had happened before. I had learned to never leave his side—too many desperate searches.

After a long wait, he emerged from the bathroom. "I've got to go out to the car. I'll see you there. I pissed the front of my pants." He started for the front door. He could never find our car in the parking lot. But with the cart full of unpaid groceries, I couldn't follow him out the door. HIGH NERVES!

"Here, you push the cart. I'm tired. It'll cover up your pants," I said. Reluctantly, he turned from the door and jerked the handle of the cart from me. The next hurdle was to get his credit card. Yesterday at his check-up at the hospital, he had had to show his insurance and Medicare cards. With his wallet a total jumble of over fifty cards, mostly expired or useless, he fumbled at least ten minutes while the account clerk waited impatiently. He took all of them out and went through them one-by-one, several times. I spotted the insurance card in the shuffle and grabbed it, then reached in and retrieved the Medicare card. He jerked the wallet away, and swatted my hand as I handed the cards to the clerk. Cards flew and spewed onto the floor, but she was able to retrieve them. He went into a loud screaming rant at me as she copied and returned them. He shoved all the cards haphazardly in with his bills. At the time, I'd thought, *Oh well, it's a hospital; she's probably seen this before.* But we were in a mall now, not the hospital. After much arguing, dropping some cards on the floor, handing me his driver's license by mistake, we found the credit card.

Check-out accomplished, we headed out the door. When I stopped to say "hello" to some neighbors in the parking lot, Andy wandered off in the opposite direction of the car. I quickly excused myself to catch up. He argued loudly as I tried to head him in the direction of the car. Then it started raining. Once we reached the car, he insisted on unlocking the lift with his key, refusing the automatic buttons. Groceries loaded, he pushed the cart to the corral and accidently set off the car's panic button. Then he pulled out his wallet and announced he had decided to organize his wallet. A few cards fell down into a nearby puddle on the pavement. In bedroom slippers, wet pants and cards falling out, he screamed at me for being bossy. I picked up the cards, making sure none were left behind, opened the car door, and forced him in. I was exhausted. Another hurdle: forcing him to buckle up.

On the drive home, Andy gave constant instructions: "Go! It's green! Swerve! Are you trying to get us killed?!" All screamed at a frantic pitch.

Lessons learned in that one outing: always check to make sure Andy is wearing shoes when we head from home, get my own credit card, have a minimal list, and stick to it. Most important on the list, get my own credit card. Also, very important, first and foremost, remember that beneath the petulant child, somewhere in there, is my dearly-loved, brilliant Andy. Beloved beyond belief and totally due my respect and love.

I recalled happier times before I lost Andy to the Land of Forgetfulness. On a guided journey through England and Scotland, our tour group stayed at an antiquated hotel deep in Scotland. We were fascinated with the stone fences that extended for miles over steep hills and deep valleys. The fences restrained thousands of sheep. It was lambing season and it seemed as though a tiny white fluff of wool tripped along beside its mother everywhere we looked. The hotel was constructed entirely of wood, no elevators, with ancient wool Tartan-patterned carpeting on the stairs and hallways. The hotel was altogether charming, with a fireplace warming the large parlor off the dining room. Surprising amenities in the huge bathroom included a heated towel rack and a heated pants holder: a device that creased pants overnight. Andy was almost fanatic in keeping a crease in his pants and in our travels often unfolded the ironing board and used the hotel clothes iron to keep his clothes pressed and presentable. This heated device that held his pants overnight and assured a sharp crease totally delighted him, and he vowed to try to duplicate it when we got back home.

I should mention I did not share Andy's enthusiasm for ironing and sharp creases. Actually, I hadn't used a clothes iron since the day I'd acquired an electric clothes dryer, about twenty years ago. I just whisked clothes from the dryer the instant they were dry and hung them up before wrinkles developed. However, I did appreciate the idea of hot towels.

We walked around the tiny Scottish town and were charmed by a stone bridge over a flowing river, so calm and peaceful we could hear the river murmuring below. Andy and I both wore heavy coats against the chill wind. "Isn't this a nice change from big city hustle and bustle?" Andy remarked as we sat in a small park near the river that curled through the town.

"Let's face it, Andy, we're both country bumpkins. This is our kind of town. No people, no traffic. The hotel is the only business in town." We were further entranced watching the magnificent sunset reflected off the river.

"We never asked when dinner is served. Maybe we should head back," Andy said, holding me in a tight hug. "Never let it be said we didn't smooch in Scotland." And smooch we did.

Later, we were summoned to the dining room by the antique bell rung by our rotund, rosy-cheeked host. We sat expectantly waiting for our meal. Instead of food coming from the kitchen, we heard voices – louder and louder voices; then the loud banging of pots and pans. We could hear metal bouncing off the walls. Andy asked, "Could they be throwing pots at each other?" It was a good guess as the banging grew louder and louder. Voices grew louder and louder.

We heard a screamed, "Alright, you SOB, the kitchen is yours! Good luck." This was followed by retreating footsteps and the loud slam of a door.

Andy grabbed my hand under the table. I could feel a vibration. I looked at him, and sure enough, he was shaking with laughter and trying to contain it to no avail. Soon the whole table was rocking with laughter. We quickly restrained ourselves when the owner, now waiter, pushed through the swinging doors. Gone was the impressive wool sports coat, replaced by a huge white apron. A big platter with a gigantic piece of unsliced roast beef was held in both hands. Smiling, he struggled with it briefly, then dropped it onto the table. "There'll be a slight delay in supper, but don't worry everything is under control. Just have patience, only a slight delay." Several trips later, the table was laden with a big bowl of unpeeled, hot potatoes, a platter with a huge quarter of a hot, very large cabbage surrounded by carrots and a loaf of unsliced bread. He stood back and surveyed the spread then scurried back into the kitchen. The doors banged open and he returned with a sharp butcher knife and four big tablespoons, laid them on the table and retreated back to the kitchen.

Andy looked around the table, his eyes still sparkling with overwhelming mirth. "Hand me that knife and I'll do the honors." With that, he sliced the beef and passed the platter. Some of the others began passing platters and in high spirits we enjoyed the feast. When the owner brought out an uncut, white frosted cake, one of the ladies wiped off the knife and sliced the cake. Being pushy Americans, a few asked for coffee. The owner shrugged and admitted he didn't know how to make it.

"I do," Jack, one of our tour buddies volunteered. "I used to run a restaurant, and nobody could make coffee to my taste." With that, he went into the kitchen, and soon we were enjoying the aroma of freshly made coffee.

We were told the tour bus was leaving at 8 a.m. sharp. We sank into the soft beds and into a deep sleep. Next morning, the bleak courtyard outside our window was transformed into a crystal fairyland. An overnight snowfall had covered tree branches, cobblestones, and buildings into dazzling, sparkling jewels. "Oh Andy, come look. A winter wonderland!" We wrapped ourselves in blankets and sat on the balcony, just drinking in the view. Calm, peace, and astounding beauty surrounded us.

"It's almost seven," Andy exclaimed. "I wonder if Jack will have to make the coffee?"

Freshly shaved, with a hint of spicy shave lotion, Andy was bandbox ready with his 4-button sports coat, gold-toed socks inside his well-polished shoes and collared sports shirt. And, yes, the crease machine did its job with a crease that was knife sharp. My handsome husband, I couldn't resist giving him a long kiss of approval.

A virtual feast was laid out on the dining room table: beans and franks, hot cinnamon buns, huge bowls of hot cereal, several coffeepots and big teapots. Most amazing was a square foot of uncapped honey still in the comb. We heard a contented hum from the kitchen, even a few snatches of song. Whatever the dispute had been, it was obviously settled. We were treated to a royal Scottish breakfast.

"Want to bet this is the most sumptuous breakfast this place has ever served?" Andy said. I drizzled a golden stream of honey on my hot biscuit. "No taker here. He's making up for last night's fiasco."

Andy helped himself to a generous chunk of honey. "I'm sorry I got everybody laughing, I just couldn't control myself." I stirred my coffee, "I don't think it was so bad. After all, we were a hungry, tired bunch. If we hadn't exploded in laughter, it could have been anger – and hungry people can get very grouchy. It could have been ugly."

Yes, happier times, indeed, when my well-groomed Andy was always on the brink of a hearty laugh.

# Chapter Ten

## Nursing Home

I've heard the phrase "a godsend" tossed around. Now I experienced it first-hand. My son, Walter, and his wife, Brenda, moved from frozen New York State to the balmy beaches of Florida. Only four miles from our house, their close proximity was truly a godsend. The dictionary describes a godsend as "anything unexpectedly needed or desired that comes at the opportune moment, as if sent by God." I remembered too, a promise the Lord gave me in a stress-filled crisis, "I will not abandon you or fail to help you. Be strong and of good courage." *(Joshua 1:5).*

The presence of Walter and Brenda lifted my overwhelming loneliness. Drinking a mug of mint tea with Brenda and having a real adult conversation was like a balm. Walt walked for miles with Andy, both at the beach and through the woods. Andy loved walking and Walt was a dear, familiar companion. Yes, they were truly a godsend.

At 3 a.m. one morning, Andy was shaking my shoulder to wake me up. *Why do these crises always happen when I'm sleeping soundest?* Barely awake, I could see he was shaking uncontrollably – body, hands, even his teeth were chattering. Alarmed, I bolted up, "Let me get you some hot tea." I assumed he was cold. I settled him on a chair in the living room and soon had the hot tea. He was shaking so violently he couldn't get even a sip, tea spilling down his pajamas and onto his lap. With growing alarm, I quickly dressed, pulled a warm robe around Andy and called Walt for help in getting Andy into the car.

An alert emergency room attendant brought out a wheelchair and helped Andy into it. I hastily parked the car while Walter accompanied Andy inside. When I arrived minutes later, he was on a gurney and surrounded by three attendants taking his vitals and questioning him. He was barely able to speak through the shaking. Bewildered, he answered their questions, "I was coughing and coughing and I got some cough syrup and drank it." I had already given them a list of his prescriptions, but the cough syrup was new to me.

The doctor who appeared to be in charge nodded, "Yes, with his heart medications, he'd get this reaction from cough syrup." Addressing Andy, he assured him. "Just relax, we know exactly how to help you." Giving rapid-fire instructions to a nearby nurse, he listened to heartbeat and pulse.

I couldn't read the doctor's face, was this serious, or just another bump in the road? I tried to think where he might have found cough syrup – I thought I had removed all hazards from the bathroom. How had I missed such an obvious thing as a bottle of cough syrup?

The nurse returned with a hypodermic syringe and injected his arm so expertly, he barely noticed. Within minutes the shaking subsided and his color returned to a rosy flush. I began to gather up my purse and his bathrobe. "I guess we can go home now." The doctor held out a restraining hand. "No, I want to keep him a day or two to monitor any reactions. You go home and get some sleep. I'll take it from here."

Walter and I drove home just as the sun rose. Back home in the bathroom, I wondered how I'd messed up on the cough syrup. It was soon obvious: Andy's travel shaving kit was unzipped on the counter with a half-empty bottle of cough syrup next to it. Usually kept in the very back of the closet, he'd ferreted it out in the wee hours. Of all the things he couldn't remember – who I am, where we are, what day it is, what year it is – he remembered there was cough syrup in his travel case in the back of the closet. Sometimes his memory was better than mine.

The next day, Walter came to the hospital with me as we assumed he'd be released. I needed Walt's help when driving, as Andy would suddenly open the door, threatening to "get out and walk because you drive so dangerously."

As we entered his room, it was obvious Andy was agitated. "I tried to walk home last night and they kept stopping me." Just then a nurse came in, "Yes, we had to chase him up and down the halls all night. It took all six of us to keep him in his bed. He's a handful." I could attest to that.

When Dr. P came in to evaluate Andy, I inquired about when he could go home. Dr. P answered, "He's not going home. I will only release him to a nursing home. It took all of the nurses to keep up with him. Once, he got to the exit doors and it took two burly interns to keep him from getting out the door. He's too much for you to cope with at this point. Choose one. I'll release him to a nursing home only. Let me know." With that, he left. Walter and I just looked at each other. Where would we go from there?

When the nurse came in, she gave me a list of nursing homes and phone numbers. I arranged for an interview with the administrator of a nursing home just across the street. It was a very short interview. When she heard he was a "wanderer," she closed her notepad and announced, "We don't admit wanderers." She picked up her briefcase and left.

Wow! When you're too sick for a nursing home, where do you go? To a nurse, of course. Our faithful nurse, Mary, pointed out the window to a row of low buildings half a block away. "Walk over there. If you're lucky, they'll have a vacancy. They're equipped with lockdown so Alzheimer's patients can't wander."

Walter and I entered the pleasant office. It seemed more like a private home than an institution and didn't have that repulsive hospital smell. Yes! They had a vacant room and he could be admitted that day. Walter had notified Andy's son, Karl, when Andy went into the hospital. Always supportive, Karl took the next plane from New York to Florida and was at the hospital when we returned an hour later.

Karl and Walter left to transport Andy's lift chair, family pictures, familiar bedspread and other homelike features to make the move less traumatic for him. When Andy was released later that afternoon, it looked almost like his bedroom at home. There was even a sleigh bed. The facility was laid out in a home-like atmosphere. The dining room had several round tables, each with four to six chairs. Andy's bedroom was spacious with a large bathroom, closet, and a mini fridge in the room.

As Brenda and I were smoothing sheets on the bed, a nurse's aide came in. She introduced herself as Olympia. "I'll be Andy's caregiver. Let me do a quick check of his meds with you." Olympia was very tall, almost regal. I was pleased to note no starched white uniform and thankfully no dancing teddy bears on her smock. Dressed conservatively in slacks and a modest top, she exuded an air of competence and kindness. I felt I could trust her to handle Andy's best interest. She pulled a small notebook from her pocket. "Does he shower by himself?"

I rolled my eyes, "Yes. But the only problem is he will shower several times a day. That's something to be aware of."

Olympia went down her list of questions and when his meds were in question she told me, "Dr. P comes here almost daily and I'll coordinate with him. The drug store delivers here so you'll no longer have to pick them up." Satisfied she had the basics, she shook my hand and assured me, "He'll be just fine. I'll keep a close eye on him. Most residents adjust quickly." I felt comfortable that Andy was in good, competent hands with Olympia.

Andy didn't question his new surroundings. He was delighted and happy to see Karl – his presence was a great joy to Andy. He dearly loved his two sons, Karl and Ed. It was always a high holiday when they visited him. I left them comfortably chatting, laughing and, as always, remembering thirty or forty years ago, which was clear as a bell to Andy. "Remember that camping trip when a whole band of raccoons stampeded past the tent in the night?" They both laughed at the remembrance and launched into other camping exploits as I tiptoed out without goodbyes. I went home and slept the clock around, six to six, my first uninterrupted sleep in years.

When I arrived next morning at eight, Andy was shaved, showered and dressed, ready for breakfast. I accompanied him to the dining room where there were twelve other "residents" – all women. Andy smiled and loudly said, "Good morning" – in Finnish. I drank coffee while he ate a substantial breakfast, with several coffee fill-ups. Back in his room, he remarked, "What a cold bunch of Finns. Did you notice not one of them greeted me back." Of course not, he'd greeted them in Finnish.

Karl stayed several days and spent most of each day with Andy at the nursing home. Andy so loved his company he never once questioned his new surroundings. I made a brief visit each day and could hear them laughing and talking from way down the hall as I approached. There was a wonderful outdoor walkway and they spent much time walking and talking.

Through deft questioning it was clear Andy thought I was Milli and we were in a Finnish hotel. Not a nursing home. Throughout his stay, he was on a fun trip to Finland and full of the excitement of the trip. "Milli, let's go to that great restaurant we found near the North Pole."

Never arguing, I said, "A great idea! Karl's coming later, let's go after he leaves." As though on cue, Karl arrived and I left as Karl planned to spend the day. Thankfully, Karl could stay several days. The day he left, Andy's other son Ed arrived. He stayed four days and so the first week hurdle was over. During the pleasant and happy time with his dearly loved sons, the conversations centered around Andy's career days and the childhood days of the boys. They seemed never to be at a loss for conversation recalling Ed's teenage adventures and misadventures.

None of the begging to come home, hating to see me leave or other horrors I'd anticipated ever happened. However, I experienced deep guilt because of Andy's being in a nursing home and when anyone inquired about Andy, I went into great detail that it was the doctor's decision that he go there, not mine. My dream of keeping Andy at home "no matter what" was unrealistic and undoable. The criteria of a danger to self or others clearly existed. I could not keep him from wandering no matter how diligently I watched. However, I did have a lot of guilt until I realized how happy Andy was in his new surroundings.

The first day I arrived after his sons left, Olympia caught up with me going down the hall to Andy's room. "We had a slight mishap last night," she told me. "As you warned me, Andy took a shower before he went to bed and left the shower running. I noticed when water ran under his door and out into the hall. His rug is still pretty soaked and we dried it out with fans. He spent some time in the dayroom watching TV, but he's back in his room now and everything is dried out."

"Oh no. You had to clean up all that water?"

Olympia didn't appear to be upset, "Hey, believe me I've cleaned up worse. Actually, Andy slept throughout the cleanup. He's a sound sleeper and even the water vac didn't wake him up. As incidents go, it was pretty uneventful."

I found him dressed, showered, and shaved, propped upright with pillows on the bed with a pad and pencil on a third pillow. He appeared distracted by my entrance, held up his hand, and said, "Give me a minute, I'm still working on the schedule."

*Land of Forgetfulness*

Watching as he wrote industrially on his pad, I asked, "What schedule?" as I put snacks and a sandwich in the tiny fridge. With a vigorous dismissal of his hand he replied impatiently, "The order the athletes line up for the Olympics."

Well, this beat my dreaded anticipation of begging to go home. I started to sit down and he protested, "Why don't you go sightseeing. This is probably your only chance to explore Japan. The buildings are spectacular, very unusual. I spotted a few riding here in the limo. Go out and explore the city. You can see, I'll be tied up here for hours." I shrugged, "You're right, I'll see you later." At this point I'd learned the best answer to any situation was, "You are right."

The cook, Debra, a regal, brown goddess, was indeed queen of the kitchen. Caring and wise, she always made a pot of coffee for Andy and me when I arrived. A woman with a no-nonsense attitude, she joined me with my cup. She shared with me that she prayed daily for each of the thirteen residents. "Does Andy seem to be adjusting?" I asked.

She rolled her expressive brown eyes. "Oh my, yes! I'd say very well. That man is like a rooster in the hen house. As you know the other twelve residents are all women and they all rush to sit with him at meals. He's assigned to this table here, but there's a general push and shove to sit with Andy. The two women assigned to sit here have to come early to assure their places. Oh yes, I'd say he's adjusting all right. There's no doubt he enjoys meal times. Plus, he has a good appetite, eats every bite. Sometimes I give him seconds."

As I left to return to the room, I glanced at my watch. I'd been gone a half-hour, per the usual attention span of about 20 minutes. *He's probably back from Japan by now.* But he was still attentive to pad and pencil, annoyed that I'd come back and distracted him. "Why don't you just go back to the hotel room and read or something? I won't be able to explore the city with you for hours. Can't you see I'm busy here?"

I made eye contact. "You're right, Andy, I'll see you later." A good day to go home and catch up.

Just as Andy loved being with his sons, I equally loved being with my daughters, Cheryl and Shelly. They'd arrived from frozen New York the day Ed left. They loved and respected Andy and spent time with him the better part of each day. We all walked the half-block-long sidewalk in the fenced-in perimeter of the nursing home. That day, we estimated we'd all walked about two miles up and down the long sidewalk. Their visit was at the end of Andy's second week at the nursing home. The girls went home to pack and I went to the dining room with Andy, very early as his table-mates, Naomi and Velma, were already there, holding their places.

"It's such fun since Andy came," Velma told me. "He keeps us in stitches. He has a joke for anything we mention. Sometimes we can barely eat, we are laughing so hard." Naomi agreed, "The tears actually run down our cheeks, we laugh so hard."

Right on cue, Andy launched into what was for me, an old familiar joke. He could recall all of his old jokes, including every nuance. Of all things forgotten, not those old jokes. Like butter rising to the top of cream, these old canards rose to the top. How the ladies loved them. Of course they hadn't heard them over and over. They told me with wonder, "He has a million jokes." He launched another one. As I let myself out, I glanced back and sure enough, I saw tears running down their cheeks, Andy's included. Out on the sidewalk, headed to my car, I could still hear their laughter.

Driving down the long, tree-shaded driveway, a long-cherished verse of scripture came to mind: "Now unto Him that is able to do exceeding abundantly above all that we ask, or even think according to the power that works in us." *(Ephesians 3:20, KJV)*. Yes, I had to admit, my puny prayer that Andy wouldn't beg to come home had been answered "abundantly" above what I could even think — that Andy would actually enjoy the nursing home.

The last night of Cheryl and Shelly's visit, we treated ourselves to a festive dinner at Fernandina's PLAE, our favorite restaurant *(People Laughing And Eating)*. We remarked on how well Andy adjusted to his new phase of life, and how well suited that nursing home was to him.

Their cases packed and lined up at the front door for an early morning start, we settled in for a good night's sleep. The shrill of the phone woke us all up at midnight. Olympia was telling me Andy had suffered some sort of attack and had been taken to the emergency room of the hospital.

# Chapter Eleven
## At the Hospital

I jerked awake from much-needed sleep to the loud ringing of the phone. I fumbled for the phone that was interrupting my dream and pressed the receiver to my ear. I heard Olympia's frantic voice, "So sorry, but we had to take Mr. Andy to the emergency room at the hospital. The ambulance has already delivered him."

I interrupted her, "What happened?"

"I'm not sure, he turned blue, actually purple around his lips. He appeared to experience a heart problem, that's when I realized he should be in a hospital."

"Thanks Olympia, we'll go immediately." I alerted Cheryl and Shelly. We were hastily dressed and on the road to the hospital within minutes of Olympia's call. I experienced a strong déjà vu. Driving through the deserted streets at midnight, headed to the bedside of a loved one took me back so many years ago to my father's bedside. The only difference between the midnight rides was that then, we were leaving the hospital, not heading to it as we were now.

That long ago midnight-ride was on Halloween, when I was only ten-years old and my father thirty-eight. Ghosts and eerie figures appeared briefly in our headlights. We were returning home after my dear father died.

I recalled that long, very hot summer I'd kept vigil on what, even at ten, I'd realized were my father's last days. His once robust body had been shrunken by cancer to a skeletal eighty pounds. Even his surroundings had shrunken to a single bed on the first floor from his spacious second floor huge bed. One day his doctor, Dr. Impert – a friend as well as his doctor – came from his small bedroom, tears streaming down his face. He carried a milk pail of fluid recently drained from my dear daddy. He mumbled, half to himself, half to me, "I think Charlie needs surgery. This has gone on too long."

A few days later, Daddy died on the operating table. On that grisly Halloween ride home, I remember thinking, "This is the worst thing to ever happen. If I can live through this, I can live through anything." Riding the midnight streets with my dear daughters, I feared that grisly dance of death could be ahead of us.

Looking back over the past eight years, I saw them as years of deep sadness, despair, and diminishment. I had been advised at the beginning that Alzheimer's was terminal. I found myself asking, *Why?* I was convinced that our tears are never wasted. Hurtling through the midnight streets, I perceived a possible answer as the Lord reminded me that He is "…the God of all comfort, who comforts us in all our tribulation, that we may be able to comfort them who are in any trouble, by the comfort wherewith we ourselves are comforted of God." *(2 Corinthians 1:4, KJV).* The tight constriction around my heart eased somewhat as I recalled that we can be positive. "God will tenderly comfort you." *(2 Corinthians 4:7, KJV).* As we entered the hospital, I sent up a prayer asking for strength and the Lord's tender comfort.

As we entered his cubicle at the emergency room, Andy looked up, "We're in France, aren't we?" By now I was accomplished at humoring his fantasies, "Yes, this is France."

"I thought so. I heard all the bells and whistles. These streets are so noisy. Always sirens, bells, and whistles. Probably the noisiest city in the world." With that, Andy closed his eyes and appeared to sleep.

On our very first appointment, Dr. P had looked at me pointedly and declared, "Realize Alzheimer's is a terminal disease. The progression escalates until the patient is in a fetal position, unable to swallow or breathe, which eventually leads to death. Do you understand? This is a terminal disease."

Later, at an Alzheimer's caregivers meeting, a distraught woman recounted a relative's long-drawn out diminishment from starvation. Three long months after the family opted not to have a feeding tube inserted, she finally died. A doctor had explained to the family that a feeding tube could postpone the inevitable as much as a year. They made the compassionate, difficult decision to do nothing. I very much feared the possibility of having to make that awful decision. I too resolved against a feeding tube as Andy and I had discussed years earlier to make no last ditch efforts in the event of life or death decisions.

We were led to a large private room with a pullout couch, a few chairs, and dear Andy looking surprisingly calm, settled in bed. Once settled in the room, I held his hand. He looked at me, "Oh, Lorraine, I'm so glad you're here."

What? Lorraine? For the first time in four years, he knew me. Called me by name! His eyes registered recognition. My thoughts instantly rearranged, from expecting the death knell, to, "Oh, he's so much better. He knows me, he knows me. He must be getting better."

He reached out and clasped my hand, holding it firmly. "The years we've been together have been the happiest of my life."

What? He recalls past years? This brilliant person so debilitated the past four years that he couldn't sort out day, month or year time sequences? He had a slight smile on his face. "Remember that ostrich that took a liking to me in Australia and followed us all day?"

My heart flared with hope for the first time in years. Was it possible my dearly loved companion was restored to me? Andy: witty and brilliant with a quirky snobbish side. That side that revered four-button cuffs, his penchant for gold-toe socks. I recalled the showy side that relished the look of astonishment when he tipped with a $50 bill. The same Andy who walked four to five miles a day as routine? Was it possible he was being restored to his past brilliance? It seemed more and more likely. He would doze momentarily and about every four or five minutes gaze at me with full recognition, say my name, and recount a past, loved memory. "I still recall that mad scramble we had to get out of the Bay of Fundy before the water overtook us. And after all the warnings we'd received."

I added, "Yes, the tour guide told us over and over that the bay fills up quickly and deeply. He said, 'Don't linger. It's dry one minute and chest-high a few minutes later.'"

Andy chuckled, "We were so busy studying the rock strata and soil formations we completely forgot all the warnings."

Remembering, I said, "How we scrambled up that steep bank. I was so afraid we wouldn't make it."

Andy added, "When we got to the top, how everyone cheered. They all cheered, then I started laughing and pretty soon everybody was roaring with laughter."

"I know," I said. "We were so relieved we'd made it to the top I think it was pure nerves that made us laugh so long."

Andy clasped my hand firmly. "We've had such fun haven't we?"

I agreed, and kept a firm grip on his hand. I was flooded with joy. Then remembering where we were and why, I asked, "Are you in any pain?"

"I'm not in pain, but my right side just feels funny," he said. "Doesn't hurt, but just feels funny." Nurses were in and out often and giving him shots regularly. He dozed off and on and often recalled other sweet memories. "Those precious days just sitting on the porch, enjoying the view. The day those twin fawns played on the lawn right in front of us, their mother stamping her foot for them to leave and they just romped and played so near us. One fawn with the white spots of a newborn and the other was snow white. They were so unafraid of us and chased each other and played while their mother stamped and stamped from the edge of the woods."

I sat astounded as memory after memory was retrieved clear and concise. The tight constriction around my heart disappeared as he recalled past events and often repeated, "The years of our marriage are some of the happiest times of my life."

My joy increased as several memories surfaced while Andy recalled incidents from eight to ten years before. He recalled a horse that peed over and over on a buggy ride we'd taken on Prince Edward Island. We both laughed as he remembered how he and two teenaged boys had rocked the buggy with their laughter as the horse seemed never to give up the flow. I chided him, "You rascal, you encouraged those boys to laugh."

Andy squeezed my hand. "Guilty. We've had some fun, quirky times, haven't we?" For a minute, he had that old gleam in his eyes.

I sat through the night in a happy daze, sure he was being restored to his former self. Shelly and Cheryl were more alert to the fact that he was given morphine shots every hour. I was so overwhelmed with joy at what I believed was restoration, that I wasn't even aware the shots were morphine.

Several times when he seemed restless, I laid hands on him, "Dear Lord, give Andy your peace." Each time I prayed, he raised his left hand in praise, "Yes, Lord! Yes, Lord!"

At about 3 a.m., I left the room briefly to get a cup of coffee. Cheryl and Shelly were nearby on the pullout couch, giving me much needed moral support. I motioned Shelly to come hold Andy's hand as he dozed. I left for coffee.

Andy opened his eyes, "Shelly, where's your mother?" In the past week he hadn't known Shelly, much less that I was her mother. In fact for the past four years he'd often asked who she was. She was astonished he knew her after years of inquiry of who she was.

"She just went for coffee," she replied

As I resumed my chair by his side, he reached for my hand. "Oh good! You're back. I'm still remembering those lovely, peaceful days on the porch, drinking coffee, the peaceful quiet, and the view. Oh, and the day that bear passed through the yard. Just huge, and so black he shown blue in the sunlight."

I sat there utterly astounded. "What is happening? Is my dear, brilliant companion being restored to me?" When he stirred restlessly, I asked again if he was in pain.

He answered, "No, but my whole right side just feels funny. No pain, but it just feels funny, just feels different." A nurse came in every hour and gave him another morphine shot. It made him drowsy, but he was in and out of sleep, always recalling with joy and humor some incident in the past. Incidents from the past! This from a man who only a few hours previously didn't know who I was. No wonder I experienced such joy.

Our bedside vigil began at midnight. At six in the morning, Dr. P came in. To me it had hardly seemed more than an hour from midnight to morning, as I was so overjoyed at his restored memory. I eagerly asked the doctor what the prognosis was.

He looked at me pityingly. "There is no prognosis. Only a fourth of his heart is still functioning. I've never known anyone to live even an hour after that massive a heart attack."

I tried to assimilate this new information. This was the first I'd been told that only a fourth of his heart was still functioning. For the first time, it washed over me that he was dying. My emotions had to adjust from "he's being restored to his former astute self" to "he's dying." It was such a total abrupt shift, I almost couldn't take it in.

Then the doctor said, "From the heartbeat, it's minutes now, not hours." Soon after, Andy took his last breath…peacefully.

Later, I realized that the last six hours were a pure gift from the Lord. Instead of the heart wrenching wondering if he still hated me, as he'd so often shouted, I had the six hours of repeated assurance that our years together were some of the happiest times of his life. The laughter we'd shared in the "good days" when he'd been the *real* Andy were true and real. It is rare – to almost never – for an Alzheimer's patient to regain total recall as Andy did. It is not an expected outcome. How precious that the Lord sometimes rewards us with an unexpected, totally unexplained occurrence.

And the Lord proved true and real. A promise I'd clutched to my heart through the dark days: "You have let me sink down in desperate problems. But you will bring me back to life again…you will turn again and comfort me." *(Psalm 71:20)*. Yes, what more concrete comfort could I seek than Andy saying over and over, "Those were the happiest years of my life."

I remembered, "How greatly to be envied are those you have chosen to come and live with you within the holy tabernacle courts! What joys await us among all the good things there." *(Psalm 65:4)*. I noted that the scripture put joy in the plural, joys. I also remembered this wonderful comfort, "The joy of the Lord is your strength." *(Nehemiah 8:1)*.

# Epilogue

# Two Years Later

Searching for a missing earring, I opened a seldom-used jewelry box. There was a sealed envelope with my name on it. I opened it and read this:

June 11, 2002

Dearest Lorraine,
   On this the eighth anniversary of our first date, I wish to tell you how happy you have made me. There will be no attempt to produce a literary work. Just honest words experienced by a man who loves you.

- You look on the bright cheerful side of most events.
- You are a Christian in the true sense as much as this is possible in an imperfect world.
- You are an exciting woman in bed, very feminine and so sexy that you sparkle and shine. (a joy forever)
- You are kind, generous and forgiving.
- You are a superb cook who prepares feasts on a near daily basis.
- You love to read and enjoy quiet time as a natural part of living.
- You are considerate of my children and grandchildren.
- You study proper health as it relates to diet, exercise, and management of stress to the benefit of those around you.
- You run a relaxed home where I feel welcome.
- You are a good money manager, even though you remind me that you gave up your pension benefits to marry me.

- You are an attractive, well-groomed and well-dressed woman who I love to be seen in the company of. I list this near the bottom because you say I relate physical beauty too highly.

This is only a partial list of your good qualities.

All my love,

Andy

P.S. You love cats and eating out.

# Coping Clues

## COPING CLUES: CHAPTER ONE

- Don't argue with or correct an Alzheimer's patient. Always agree.
- Don't try to cover up that your loved one is afflicted with Alzheimer's. It has nothing to do with intelligence and was not caused by something you or your loved one did.
- Put the information your loved one regularly seeks, such as the day of the week, on a large banner prominently displayed in your home, where it can be referred to as often as needed.
- Realize formerly easy tasks may now be difficult or impossible to navigate, such as hot and cold faucets, the TV remote, dialing a phone, answering a phone, or reading a clock.
- Sundown Syndrome can sometimes be mitigated by soothing music, joining in piecing a puzzle together, or taking a walk. Any pleasant distraction may help.
- What appears to be stubbornness, such as making the same mistake over and over, may be due to forgetfulness. There is barely a 20-minute memory span.
- It is important to remember Alzheimer's is a disease of the brain, not a mental illness.

# COPING CLUES: CHAPTER TWO

- Your loved one may no longer be able to read time from a clock, which explains if they constantly ask you what time it is. Answer patiently, even if it's the tenth time this hour.
- Be aware that your loved one may no longer be able to make small repairs, have the ability to cook, or recognize fire hazards.
- Use nightlights liberally throughout the entire house.
- Make sure medications, including over the counter meds like cough syrup, are not easily accessible.
- Keep a spare key outside in case you are locked out.
- Don't leave your loved one alone with open fire, a trash fire, a fireplace or a bonfire.

## COPING CLUES: CHAPTER THREE

- There are very few warning signs of Alzheimer's disease. No one expects it.
- A once loving, considerate person may become hostile in later stages. This is important to remember when behavior deteriorates.
- Realize your loved one may no longer be able to keep track of household details the person managed before the onset of Alzheimer's, such as the household accounts, tax payments, oil changes, fertilizer schedules, etc.

## COPING CLUES: CHAPTER FOUR

- An Alzheimer's patient who has never uttered a curse word may begin to curse often. Try to ignore it when you are cursed and raged at. Be aware the "real person" isn't cursing you. Changing the subject may be the best coping method.
- If there are certain items your loved one regularly loses, build up a supply of extra replacements, such as low-cost backup wallets and glasses.
- Anticipate unexpected explosions of rage. Do not confront or try to reason with the Alzheimer's patient in these instances. The best method is to divert attention.
- Hallucinations may occur because of the complex changes in the brain that cause a loved one to see and hear things that have no basis in reality. Don't panic; distract and change the subject.
- If your loved one is sometimes in fear of imagined danger, assure them you're taking their fears seriously and try to comfort and reassure them of their safety.
- Try to keep Alzheimer's patients engaged and relaxed. Give them something to do: coloring, painting, even sorting silverware, folding laundry or matching socks.

## COPING CLUES: CHAPTER FIVE

- Remove coats, hats, and walking shoes from the front door, as they symbolize departure.
- Deadbolts or chain locks at the top of an outside door may be a hindrance to escape – or at least stall it enough for you to realize your loved one is attempting to leave.
- Another tool you may be able to use to prevent escape is a loosely-fitting doorknob covering. This will make the cover turn instead of the actual knob.
- Medical ID bracelets are available to ensure your loved one always has an address and phone number on his or her person. Some have GPS chips. Make sure they are comfortable and not easily removed. There are also GPS chips that can be placed in sneakers or hats. Local sheriff's offices can help obtain these items.
- There are floor pads available that sound an alarm when stepped on. Place them near a bed or an outside door to be alerted if a loved one is on the move at night.
- Have some form of identity on your loved one. If they resist ID bracelets, it could be something as simple as a business card or a slip of paper with name and address.
- Hospice, which is available at no cost, has a variety of helps. Their services are not just end of life, but also assistance in home health care. A nurse or doctor can make regular house calls, a chaplain can come at your request, and various equipment such as a hospital bed, walkers, etc., can be made available. They are on call day and night, 24 hours a day.
- At some point, realize your loved one can no longer be left alone, even for a few minutes.

# COPING CLUES: CHAPTER SIX

- Loss of coordination results in unexplained falling. Assist with a firm arm hold while walking or navigating steps or curbs.
- Without discussion, provide protective underwear when incontinence is perceived.
- Adult day care may be an answer for some.
- Curtail driving at all costs. Remove all keys to a safe place that is not accessible to your loved one. Check their pockets and key holders, and remember your own wallet or purse is not safe from discovery.
- In strange surroundings, accompany your loved one to the restroom and wait. A loved one is easily lost and may wander outside.
- Limit the amount of cash on your loved one. Replace larger denominations of cash with one dollar bills.
- Puzzles of 300 to 500 pieces are the most some can cope with.
- If taking showers or changing clothes becomes difficult, it may be time to get outside assistance.
- Have a recent photo available of your loved one in case you need help finding him or her. If you have a cell phone with you, make a habit of taking their picture whenever you arrive somewhere new so you'll have a photo of them in the outfit they are wearing at the time.

# COPING CLUES: CHAPTER SEVEN

- A caregiver should arrange at least one day a week away from home. A local church or a caregiver's group may be able to suggest someone to give respite for a few hours.
- Never refer to caregiving helpers as "babysitters" to your loved one.
- Search and make sure no sexual enhancement drugs are stashed away somewhere. In large doses, they could be fatal.
- Sometimes keeping a journal can be a stress reliever for caregivers.
- There is no such thing as too much help, but there *is* such a thing as not enough help.

# COPING CLUES: CHAPTER EIGHT

- In choosing a nursing home, for some, a homelike atmosphere is important. Find an atmosphere congenial to your loved one.
- Be sure you have a list of all medications available for staff.
- Check the security of the nursing facility if wandering is a problem.
- Familiarize yourself with the facility's visitation hours.
- Find out if you can take your loved one out for occasional excursions.
- Make staff aware of any allergies.
- Make your loved one's room more homelike by placing pictures of family around the room and bringing a favorite pillow, bedroom slippers, a favorite bedspread, etc.

## COPNG CLUES: CHAPTER NINE

- If your loved one has always been in charge of finances, it's time to get your *own* credit card.
- Check to make sure of proper shoes and clothing before heading out for shopping or appointments; you can no longer assume your loved one will remember.
- Never leave an Alzheimer's patient alone in a parked car.
- When shopping with your loved one, have a short list and stick to it.
- Sometimes as a caregiver, you just feel hopeless. Turn to what comforts you. This scripture was a comfort to me: "Even when we are too weak to have any faith left, HE remains faithful and will help us." *(2 Timothy 2:13)*.

# COPING CLUES: CHAPTER TEN

- It is quite common for the caregiver to be tempted sexually. Realize this is not uncommon and react as you would when your loved one was "normal."
- A loved one may make inappropriate sexual advances. Distraction and changing the subject are the best tools in these instances. Alert helpers to the possibility of a proposition.
- Avoid stimulating TV. Your loved one will often get caught up in the drama and perceive they are a part of the action.
- Remove ALL guns from the house. A caregiver can be mistaken for an intruder in the darkness.

Printed in the United States
By Bookmasters